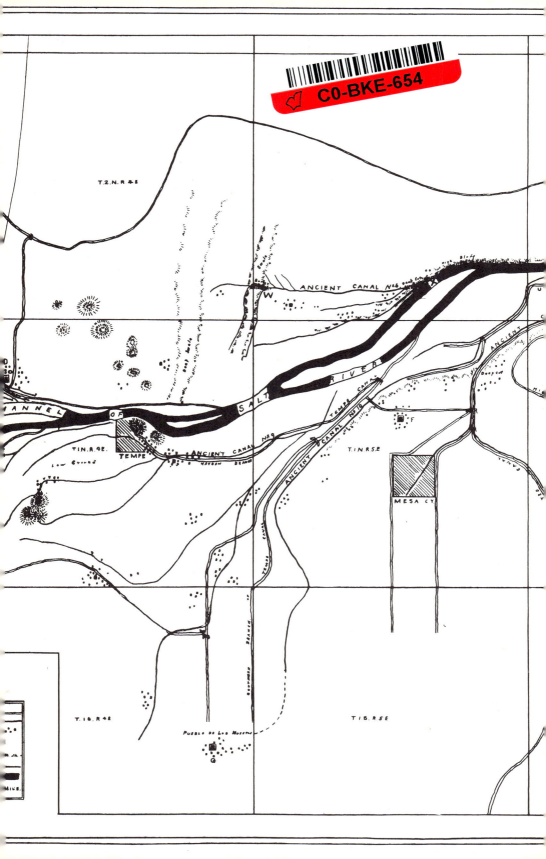

THE
LOST CITIES
OF
CIBOLA

THE
LOST CITIES
OF
CIBOLA

BY

RICHARD PETERSEN

WITH
71 PLATES & 9 FIGURES

G & H BOOKS · 2515 E. THOMAS, SUITE 16
————— PHOENIX , ARIZONA · 85016 —————

Published in the United States by

G & H Books
2515 East Thomas Rd., Suite 16
Phoenix, Arizona   85016

Manufactured in the United States of America

To the honored memory of my parents
this book is humbly dedicated.

Contents

Acknowledgements

I AM PLEASED to express my gratitude to the librarians serving the Arizona Collection at the Arizona State University for the generous help which they have offered to me on many occasions. I am also grateful to Minnabelle Laughlin of the Department of Anthropology for permitting me access to the Frank Midvale papers which are in her care. I am grateful as well to Tracy Meade, Curator of the Mesa Museum of History and Archaeology, for allowing me access to his "back room" where additional papers of Frank Midvale were still in storage, and also to Terry Hoagland, Curator of the Phoenix Museum of History, for his generous assistance and for giving me access to his source materials.

I would like to thank Pete Ferguson and Harry Holbert for sharing with me their recollections of the crosses in South Mountain Park and related matters. I am grateful also to Mireya Ehlenberger for reading and reporting upon Father Kino's discussion of the comet of 1680. The Padre wrote Spanish with a thick German flavor so the task was more difficult than it promised to be at first glance.

I am much indebted to Richard Potter for bringing to my attention the remarkable gypsum hill described in Chapter 10 and for transporting me there in his Jeep. Certainly this interesting site would otherwise not have been found. I am also pleased to acknowledge the generous assistance of Dewayne Coker during many excursions into the wilds of northwestern Arizona. These were fruitful and enlightening researches even though little shows for them explicitly in the text. I am happy to mention the help of Jerry Bledsoe and David Fields on similar occasions.

The photographs included with the text are my own unless otherwise credited. One such exception required special effort on the part of Park Ranger Ramond Olivas, so I am particularly grateful to him, and to the National Park Service, for the reproduction of the de Vargas inscription at El Morro National Monument. I would also like to express my appreciation to the Arizona Historical Foundation for allowing me to reproduce the early photgraph of the Casa Grande ruin, and to PARIS MATCH for permitting the use of their photograph of the restored moai in Plate 66.

Special thanks are due to Dr. Joseph Mastropaolo for his help in expediting production of the book and for his constant encouragement along the way.

Finally, I wish to acknowledge with deep gratitude the help of my mother, Helen Petersen, for her untiring efforts at proofreading the manuscript and for her many valuable suggestions on ways to improve it. My most profound regret is that she did not survive to see the book in print.

The first business of one who studies philosophy is to adopt an attitude of modest inquiry, since it is not possible for anyone to learn what he thinks that he already knows.

Epictetus, *ca.* A.D. 60

Prologue:

A Brief Orientation

THE ONCE-RENOWNED Cities of Cibola fell into disrepute centuries ago—so much so that apart from those who are especially concerned with the lore of early Spanish America few today have ever heard of them. In fact, History records them with such bitter disappointment that even specialists in this study area seldom mention them except in passing. That such obscure cities should now become the theme of a fair-sized volume offered to the public at large is therefore surprising and deserves a word of explanation in advance.

In the title I refer to them as the "Lost" Cities of Cibola, and so they were for I am able to show conclusively that History errs in its present drab understanding of them. In truth they were genuine cities indeed, large and populous, and they well deserved their ancient reputation. But it is not simply the error itself, nor even the correcting of it, which is to be our primary concern here—fascinating though these findings are in their own right. What removes the topic from the narrow purview of specialists and makes it worthy of broad public scrutiny is the bizarre means by which those unhappy cities came to meet their doom. For their enigmatical residues, identified and interpreted here at last, clearly reveal a heretofore unknown working of Nature, a phenomenon which staggers the imagination and would seem to be utterly beyond rational understanding. Nevertheless, by pursuing a trail of similar signs in another context some progress can be claimed, and thus we shall identify what may be the first convincing evidence for an added dimension of space.

Of course the idea of a fourth space-like dimension is far from new. It is a theme in much popular fiction, and it has been offered repeatedly as the only plausible basis for such effects as the "U.F.O. Phenomenon" and Extra-Sensory Perception. But despite the broadly based literature attesting to these phenomena and the aptness of the suggestion, the existence of a true fourth dimension has not been acknowledged in "orthodox" circles. The main reason is surely that these elusive effects cannot be reproduced under laboratory conditions where they could be examined at will. However the study at hand should go far toward overcoming this barrier, for although the phenomenon to be considered cannot be reproduced in the laboratory at least many of its bizarre, telltale residues are easily accessible to all, and we shall study some of them presently in detail.

Much is at stake here, therefore, so I would encourage the reader to test the thesis rigorously for himself from the beginning. To this end let him set aside for the moment his customary outlook on nature and declare himself free to follow the trail of evidence and the dictates of reason wherever they might lead. After having turned the last page let him look back and weigh the development in retrospect, searching for even a single false note or inconsistency. And then I would ask him to decide for himself whether any other resolution for this strange mystery would be remotely possible.

Chapter 1:

THE SEVEN CITIES

THE HOARY LEGEND of the Cities of Cibola has survived the centuries as but a shattered dream. Seven grand cities they were supposed to be, lost in the wilderness. Seven rich cities they were said to be, and thus they captured the fancies of a gold hungry world. But though the dream faded with the dawn of discovery its memory lingers on. For some strange reason writers still call it forth occasionally; they retell of it; they pronounce upon it again, and then they send it back to its musty resting place to wait for still another airing. On second thought, perhaps it's not so strange after all that the restless ghost returns to haunt us. Perhaps some sorry injustice waits to be righted. Perhaps some long hidden story remains to be told.

The cities in question first entered the flow of legitimate history shortly after the Spanish conquest of Mexico in 1521, although rumors of seven great cities "lost" somewhere in the New World had already been circulating in Spain for many years before that. Legend was that they had been founded by seven priests who had fled the Moorish oppression centuries before. Whether or not there was any genuine connection between these fabled "Cities of the Antilles" and our present topic need not concern us here. We may never know for certain, but in any case one should be aware that the Spaniards were alive to the possibility of finding such cities, so their ears were tuned for information which might disclose their whereabouts.

Three witnesses (that is, three independent witnesses) are commonly noted who gave testimony for the existence and approximate location of the missing cities—two of them ostensibly relating firsthand experience. Their descriptions were not all equally detailed, as we shall see, but they agreed in substance. However, when an expedition was organized to go and take those cities by force, they turned out to be a bitter disappointment indeed for they weren't cities at all; they proved to be but tiny Indian pueblos perched on a rock in what in now northwestern New Mexico. Nevertheless, even though they differed from the advance descriptions in every important detail, History has judged the identification certain, and the question has long since been considered closed. In size and appearance, however, these small villages were very much the same as the many others which dotted the region, so a puzzle remains despite this confident verdict. Namely, how did those *particular* little pueblos, amongst all the rest, happen to acquire such a marvelous and far-reaching reputation?

For over four hundred years the world has been content to let this mystery lie. After those directly involved in the conquest had died it was apparently of no pressing concern to anyone, and the very fact that an agreeable solution failed to appear in the normal course of events might seem proof enough that the world judged well in letting the matter rest. That is, if those modest villages had been identified in error—if such great cities as the witnesses described had actually existed—then presumably the truth would have been uncovered as the region came to be more widely explored. But in order to be useful as evidence truth must not only be uncovered it must also be properly correlated, and, as we are about to find, a series of unusual events combined to bathe the whole topic of the Seven Cities in a fog of confusion which defied even the most perceptive analysts of former times.

Most of this confusion stems from an unfamiliar working of nature, but a part bears man's mark unmistakably because the written records do not agree amongst themselves. In fact, some even appear to have been deliberately falsified, so the records alone are not sufficient to resolve the problem; some basis for interpretation and selection is also needed, and here we part company with those able historians of the past. In particular, we shall find it profitable to recognize a certain principle of ingrained character which holds that men do not change their stripes easily. Most especially, those who have been drilled in a tradition of some rigorous discipline are likely to remain true to their code even in the face of death itself. One could hardly admit this simple verity into court as evidence in its own right, but it proves to be a useful key to understanding nevertheless—one which those who passed this way before knowingly set aside. Indeed, when this new key is inserted into its proper setting, the fog lifts; fresh light illuminates the scene, and in this new light we shall have no trouble at all recognizing those cities when we come upon their barely discernible residues. But far from resolving the mystery this new insight only serves to emphasize its true proportions. For up to the present time it has been thought that these are the remains of very ancient cities indeed—cities which returned to the dust during untold centuries of abandonment, erosion and decay. But if in truth they flourished until fairly recent times then this interpretation will never do; in that case they could only have been destroyed outright by some large-scale catastrophe as yet unknown. Once this is clearly understood then definitive clues to the surprising nature of this cataclysm will be easily recognizable.

Thus what seems at first to be merely an historical curiosity becomes, on resolving it, the unique and extremely valuable key which opens still other doors beyond. It is therefore only the beginning of a long and exciting road to discovery in several widely diverse fields. Let us set out upon this road now by quickly retracing the events which led up to the conquest of that most disappointing prize: The Seven Cities of Cibola (as the world now knows them).

The earliest specific reference to those notable cities was preserved by Nuño de Guzmán, President of the first *Audiencia* in New Spain (Mexico). An Indian servant told him that as a boy he had gone with his father, who was a trader, to large cities in the north which compared in size to Mexico City itself. According to this informant they were situated forty days' travel north of his home village, which was somewhere nearby—that is, near Mexico City.

One's first thought might be that those enthusiastic accounts of Cibola originated with primitive nomads who were entirely unfamiliar with permanent housing; such people might describe even modest pueblos in glowing terms. But we see that this was not the case at all. The witness here was at ease in Mexico City so he was well acquainted with urban culture, and the President himself took the man at his word. In fact, de Guzmán assembled an army and in 1530 set out to find and conquer those cities which the Indian had described. He could not cope with the mountainous terrain so he did not get very far, but he did carve out a substantial province for himself which he called New Galicia and of which he became the first Governor. De Guzmán's treatment of natives was especially cruel, however, both during the expedition and afterwards, and it eventually got him into serious trouble as we shall see presently.

Our next word of those seven wonderful cities comes from four gaunt men who were discovered by a military patrol on the outskirts of de Guzmán's new territory in the

The Seven Cities

year 1536. They were Álvar Nuñez Cabeza de Vaca*, Andrés Dorantes, Alonzo del Castillo Maldonado and an Arabian Negro named Estéban. The latter was a slave, the property of Dorantes. These four were the sole survivors of the Narváez expedition which had set out to conquer Florida eight years before. It proved to be a misadventure from the beginning. The army was not prepared for guerrilla warfare in the wilds, so they became disorganized and did poorly against the Indians. To make matters worse their ships were lost in storms so they could not escape. Disease also took its toll. Many who did not succumb outright became too weak to resist and were executed by their foes as they were found, but for some reason these four were taken as slaves instead. After suffering unspeakable privation for six years, however, they managed to elude their masters and to work their way westward and then south into Mexico where they were finally rescued.

Although their original captors had been extremely hostile, as might be expected, those Indians whom they met further to the west were quite friendly. In fact, since their prayers for the sick seem to have been very effective, the three Spaniards acquired a reputation as powerful healers, and word of their coming preceded them along the way. The Negro made no claim as a healer, but he got along especially well with the Indians so between them they had the confidence and support of the natives throughout most of their travels. Then, finally, near the end of their journey, the Indians began to speak glowingly of marvelous cities to the north, and they even displayed various tangible items which they said had come from there.

In due course Álvar Nuñez and the others found themselves in Mexico City where they were received with

---

* *The man's name was Álvar Nuñez. His cognomen, Cabeza de Vaca, (Cow's Head) was bestowed upon an ancestor by the King to honor an act of heroism which involved the head of a cow.*

great celebrations. Bull fights were held in their honor, and they were welcomed by Hernando Cortéz himself. In their report to the Viceroy, Don Antonio de Mendoza, they naturally mentioned those large and powerful cities of which they had been told repeatedly along the way.

Mendoza was greatly interested in those reports, and he was anxious to determine if they were true. With this object in mind he tried to persuade the four, any or all, to retrace their route and attempt to find those cities, but they had other plans. Dorantes and Castillo wished to marry and settle down to a more tranquil life, while Álvar Nuñez wanted to return to Spain. To be helpful, however, Dorantes presented Estéban as a gift to the Viceroy that he might be available for such an expedition if it should ever materialize. The Negro was eager to go, but because of his station he could not be given responsibility for such an important undertaking. Someone else had to be found to lead the expedition, and Mendoza selected a priest for the job. There has been much learned conjecture about his reasons for making such a choice. They may have been largely political, as many suggest, or he may simply have known the man and had confidence in him. Whatever the case, he selected to lead the mission a Franciscan monk by the name of Marcos de Niza.

Now let us note well that this was an official under-taking; the expedition was ordered by the Viceroy, and it was a matter of the utmost gravity in the eyes of all concerned. Fray Marcos was presented with detailed written instructions, and he in turn was obliged to file a written receipt stating that he understood those instructions and promised faithfully to obey them. In effect, Marcos was to be the eyes of the King in that new territory. It was a perfectly legitimate assignment, so we have every obvious reason to believe that the Friar undertook his mission in all good faith and that he filed a true and faithful report upon its conclusion. All of those documents are matters of public record to this day.

The Seven Cities

We can do no better than to read the account of that journey as Fray Marcos wrote it. The following translation into English was prepared by Dr. Percy Baldwin for the New Mexico Historical Society [1], and it is reproduced here in its entirety with only two minor variants. Baldwin anglicized the Negro's name (Stephen of Dorantes) while retaining the name of the cities in its original form—with an accent on the first syllable. There can be no doubt that Marcos wrote the name as it was told to him, so Cíbola is surely correct. But in the following, the personal name is retained as in the original, and the place name is anglicized; that is, the accent is omitted. Furthermore, the paragraphs have been numbered so they can be referred to easily. Fray Marcos refers many times to crossing "deserts" during his trek. But one should be aware that the Spanish word, *desplobado,* is used to denote any unpopulated region whatever so it is not strictly the equal of its English counterpart. One should also know that the Spanish league was taken to be the distance a horse would normally walk in an hour, and it is usually reckoned as 3.1 miles. Five such leagues, or about 15.5 miles, were considered the normal day's travel on foot.

Figure 1 is a sketch map of the territory that we shall be considering here and in the chapters to follow. Apart from Mexico City itself, only two of the centers shown were known to be in existence in 1539, namely Compostella and Culiacán, which was called San Miguel at the time. (The modern city of Culiacán lies about thirty miles north of the site of this early Spanish settlement.) The Friar mentioned by name several of the Indian villages which he passed through, but no attempt has been made to indicate them here since their locations are, in the main, problematical.

The reader cannot fail to notice that New Galicia had a new Governor by the time Fray Marcos set out on his trek. De Guzmán's continued mistreatment of the Indians had caused him to be stripped of office and thrown into prison. The new Governor, Francisco Vázquez de Coronado, was a young man, well-born and well-married, of whom we shall hear more later. Now let us turn our attention to the third of those original testimonials for the Seven Cities—an account which was written more than eighty years before the Pilgrim Fathers anchored the "Mayflower" and set their feet upon the New World!

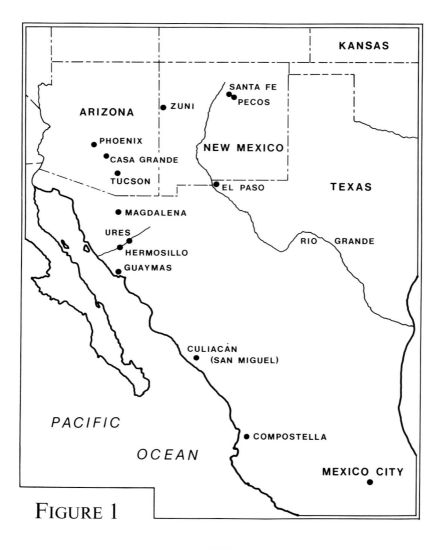

FIGURE 1

THE REPORT

OF
FRAY MARCOS DE NIZA

(1)   With the aid and favor of the most holy Virgin Mary, our Lady, and of our seraphic father, St. Francis, I, Fray Marcos de Niza, a professed religious of the order of St. Francis, in fulfillment of the instructions above given of the most illustrious lord, Don Antonio de Mendoza, viceroy and governor for H. M. of New Spain, left the town of San Miguel, in the province of Culiacán, on Friday, March 7th, 1539. I took with me as companion Friar Honoratus and also Estéban de Dorantes, a negro, and certain Indians, which the said Lord Viceroy bought for the purpose and set at liberty. They were delivered to me by Francisco de Coronado, governor of New Galicia, along with many other Indians from Petatlan and from the village of Cuchillo, situated about fifty leagues from the said town. All these came to the valley of Culiacán, manifesting great joy, because it had been certified to them that the Indians were free, the said governor having sent in advance to acquaint them of their freedom and to tell them that it was the desire and command of H. M. that they should not be enslaved nor made war upon nor badly treated.

(2)   With this company as stated, I took my way toward the town of Petatlan, receiving much hospitality and presents of food, roses and other such things; besides which, at all the stopping-places where there were no people, huts were constructed

for me of mats and branches. In this town of Petatlan I stayed three days, because my companion, Friar Honoratus, fell sick. I found it advisable to leave him there and, conformably with the instructions given to me, I followed the way in which I was guided, though unworthy, by the Holy Ghost. There went with me Estéban de Dorantes, the negro, some of the freed Indians and many people of that country. I was received everywhere I went with much hospitality and rejoicing and with triumphal arches. The inhabitants also gave me what food they had, which was little, because they said it had not rained for three years, and because the Indians of that territory think more of hiding than of growing crops, for fear of the Christians of the town of San Miguel, who up to that time were accustomed to make war upon and enslave them. On all this road, which would be about 25 or 30 leagues beyond Petatlan, I did not see anything worthy of being set down here, except that there came to me some Indians from the island visited by the Marquess of Valle, and who informed me that it was really an island and not, as some think, part of the mainland. I saw that they passed to and from the mainland on rafts and that the distance between the island and the mainland might be half a sea league, rather more or less. Likewise there came to see me Indians from another larger and more distant island, by whom I was told that there were thirty other small islands, inhabited, but with poor food excepting two, which they said had maize. These Indians wore suspended from their necks many shells of the kind which contain pearls; I showed them a pearl which I carried for sample and they told me that there were some in the islands, but I did not see any.

(3)   I took my way over a desert for four days and there went with me some Indians from the islands mentioned as well as from the villages which I left behind, and at the end of the desert I found some other Indians, who were astonished to see me, as they had no news of Christians, having no traffic with the people on the other side of the desert. These Indians

made me very welcome, giving me plenty of food, and they endeavored to touch my clothes, calling me Sayota, *which means in their language, "man from heaven." I made them understand, the best I could by my interpreters, the content of my instructions, namely, the knowledge of our Lord in heaven and of H. M. on earth. And always, by all the means that I could, I sought to learn about a country with numerous towns and a people of a higher culture than those I was encountering, but I had no news except that they told me that in the country beyond, four or five days' journey thence, where the chains of mountains ended, there was an extensive and level open tract, in which they told me there were many and very large towns inhabited by a people clothed with cotton. When I showed them some metals which I was carrying, in order to take account of the metals of the country, they took a piece of gold and told me that there were vessels of it among the people of the region and that they wear certain articles of that metal suspended from their noses and ears, and that they had some little blades of it, with which they scrape and relieve themselves of sweat. But as this tract lies inland and my intention was to stay near the coast, I determined to leave it till my return, because then I would be able to see it better. And so I marched three days through a country inhabited by the same people, by whom I was received in the same manner as by those I had already passed. I came to a medium-sized town named Vacapa, where they made me a great welcome and gave me much food, of which they had plenty, as the whole land is irrigated. From this town to the sea is forty leagues. As I found myself so far away from the sea, and as it was two days before Passion Sunday, I determined to stay there until Easter, to inform myself concerning the islands of which I said above that I had news. So I sent Indian messengers to the sea, by three ways, whom I charged to bring back to me people from the coast and from some of the islands, that I might inform myself concerning them. In another direction I sent Estéban de Dorantes, the negro, whom I instructed to take the route toward the north for fifty or sixty leagues to see if by that way he might obtain an account of any important thing such as we were seeking. I agreed with him that if he had any news of a populous, rich and important country he should not continue further but should return in person or send me Indians with a certain signal which we arranged, namely, that if it were something of medium importance, he should send me a white cross of a hand's breadth, if it were something of great importance, he should send me one of two hands' breadth, while if it were bigger and better than New Spain, he should send me a great cross. And so the said negro Estéban departed from me on Passion Sunday after dinner, whilst I stayed in the town, which as I say is called Vacapa.*

(4)   In four days' time there came messengers from Estéban with a very great cross, as high as a man, and they told me on Estéban's behalf that I should immediately come and follow him, because he had met people who gave him an account of the greatest country in the world, and that he had Indians who had been there, of whom he sent me one. This man told me so many wonderful things about the country, that I forbore to believe them until I should have seen them, or should have more certitude of the matter. He told me that it was thirty days' journey from where Estéban was staying to the first city of the country, which was named Cibola. As it appears to me to be worth while to put in this paper what this Indian, whom Estéban sent me, said concerning the country, I will do so. He asserted that in the first province there were seven very great cities, all under one lord, that the houses, constructed of stone and lime, were large, that the smallest were of one story with a terrace above, that there were others of two and three stories, whilst that of the lord had four, and all were joined under his rule. He said that the doorways of the principal houses were much ornamented with turquoises, of which there was a great abundance, and that the people of those cities went very well clothed. He told me many particulars,

not only of the seven cities but of other provinces beyond them, each one of which he said was much bigger than that of the seven cities. That I might understand the matter as he knew it, we had many questions and answers and I found him very intelligent.

(5)   I gave thanks to Our Lord, but deferred my departure after Estéban de Dorantes, thinking that he would wait for me, as I had agreed with him, and also because I had promised the messengers whom I had sent to the sea that I would wait for them, for I proposed always to treat with good faith the people with whom I came in contact. The messengers returned on Easter Sunday, and with them people from the coast and from two islands, which I knew to be the islands above mentioned, and which, as I already knew, are poor of food, though populated. These people wore shells on their foreheads and said that they contain pearls. They told me that there were thirty-four islands, near to one another, whose names I am setting down on another paper, where I give the names of the islands and towns. The people of the coast say that they, as well as the people of the islands, have little food, and that they traffic with one another by means of rafts. The coast trends almost directly toward the north. These Indians of the coast brought to me shields of oxhide, very well fashioned, big enough to cover them from head to foot, with some holes above the handle so that one could see from behind them; they are so hard, that I think that a bullet would not pass through them. The same day there came to me three of those Indians known as Pintados, *with their faces, chests and arms all decorated; they live over toward the east and their territory borders on those near the seven cities. They told me that, having had news of me, they had come to see me and among other things they gave me much information concerning the seven cities and provinces that the Indian sent by Estéban had told me of, and almost in the same manner as he. I therefore sent back the coast people, but two Indians of the islands said they would like to go with me seven or eight days.*

(6)   So with them and the three Pintados *already mentioned, I left Vacapa on the second day of the Easter festival, taking the same road that Estéban had followed. I had received from him more messengers, with another big cross as big as the first which he sent, urging me to hurry and stating that the country in question was the best and greatest of which he had ever heard. These messengers gave me, individually, the same story as the first, except that they told me much more and gave me a clearer account. So for that day, the second of Easter, and for two more days I followed the same stages of the route as Estéban had; at the end of which I met the people who had given him news of the seven cities and of the country beyond. They told me that from there it was thirty days' journey to the city of Cibola, which is the first of the seven. I had an account not from one only, but from many, and they told me in great detail the size of the houses and the manner of them, just as the first ones had. They told me that beyond these seven cities there were other kingdoms named Marata, Acus and Totonteac. I desired very much to know for what they went so far from their homes and they told me that they went for turquoises, cowhides and other things, that there was a quantity of these things in that town. Likewise I asked what they exchanged for such articles and they told me the sweat of their brows and the service of their persons, that they went to the first city, which is called Cibola, where they served in digging the ground and performing other work, for which work they are given oxhides of the kind produced in that country, and turquoises. The people of this town all wear good and beautiful turquoises hanging from their ears and noses and they say that these jewels are worked into the principal doors of Cibola. They told me that the fashion of clothing worn in Cibola is a cotton shirt reaching to the instep, with a button at the throat and a long cord hanging down, the sleeves of the shirts being the same width throughout their length; it seems to me this would resemble the Bohemian style. They say that those people go girt with*

belts of turquoises and that over these shirts some wear excellent cloaks and others very well dressed cowhides, which are considered the best clothing, and of which they say there is a great quantity in that country. The women likewise go clothed and covered to the feet in the same manner.

(7)   These Indians received me very well and took great care to learn the day of my departure from Vacapa, so that they might furnish me on the way with victuals and lodgings. They brought me sick persons that I might cure them and they tried to touch my clothes; I recited the Gospel over them. They gave me some cowhides so well tanned and dressed that they seemed to have been prepared by some highly civilized people, and they all said that they came from Cibola.

(8)   The next day I continued my journey, taking with me the Pintados, *who wished not to leave me. I arrived at another settlement, where I was very well received by its people, who also endeavored to touch my clothing. They gave me information concerning the country whither I was bound as much in detail as those I had met before, and they told me that some persons had gone from there with Estéban de Dorantes, four or five days previously. Here I found a great cross which Estéban had left for me, as a sign that the news of the good country continually increased, and he had left word for me to hurry and that he would wait for me at the end of the first desert. Here I set up two crosses and took possession, according to my instructions, because that country appeared to me better than that which I had already passed and hence it was fitting to perform the acts of possession.*

(9)   In this manner I traveled five days, always finding people, who gave me a very hospitable reception, many turquoises and cowhides and the same account of the country. They all spoke to me right away of Cibola and that province as people who knew that I was going in search of it. They told me how Estéban was going forward, and I received from him messengers who were inhabitants of that town and who had been some distance with him. He spoke more and more

enthusiastically of the greatness of the country and he urged me to hurry. Here I learned that two days' journey thence I would encounter a desert of four days' journey, in which there was no provision except what was supplied by making shelters for me and carrying food. I hurried forward, expecting to meet Estéban at the end of it, because he had sent me word that he would await me there.

(10)   Before arriving at the desert, I came to a green, well watered settlement, where there came to meet me a crowd of people, men and women, clothed in cotton and some covered with cowhides, which in general they consider a better dress material than cotton. All the people of this town wear tur-quoises hanging from their noses and ears; these ornaments are called cacona. *Among them came the chief of the town and his two brothers, very well dressed in cotton,* encaconados, *and each with a necklace of turquoises around his neck. They brought to me a quantity of game—venison, rabbits and quail—also maize and meal, all in great abundance. They offered me many turquoises, cowhides, very pretty cups and other things, of which I accepted none, for such was my custom since entering the country where we were not known. And here I had the same account as before of the seven cities and the kingdoms and provinces as I have related above. I was wearing a garment of dark woolen cloth, of the kind called* Saragossa, *which was given to me by Francisco Vázquez de Coronado, governor of New Galicia. The chief of the village and other Indians touched it with their hands and told me that there was plenty of that fabric in Totonteac, and that the natives of that place were clothed with it. At this I laughed and said it could not be so, that it must be garments of cotton which those people wore. Then they said to me: "Do you think that we do not know that what you wear and what we wear is different? Know that in Cibola the houses are full of that material which we are wearing, but in Totonteac there are some small animals from which they obtain that with which they make a fabric like yours." This astonished me, as I had*

not heard of any such thing previously, and I desired to inform myself more particularly about it. They told me that the animals are of the size of the Castilian greyhounds which Estéban had with him; they said there were many of them in Totonteac. I could not guess what species of animals they might be.

(11)   The next day I entered into the desert and at the place where I had to go for dinner I found huts and food enough by the side of a watercourse. At night I found cabins and food again and so it was for the four days that I traveled through this desert. At the end of them, I entered a very well populated valley and at the first town many men and women came with food to meet me. They all wore many turquoises suspended from their noses and ears, and some wore necklaces of turquoise, like those which I said were worn by the chief of the town on the other side of the desert, and his brothers, except that they only wore one string, while these Indians wore three or four. They were dressed in very good cloaks of ox leather. The women likewise wore turquoises in their noses and ears and very good petticoats and blouses. Here they had as much information of Cibola, as in New Spain they have of Mexico and in Peru of Cuzco. They described in detail the houses, streets and squares of the town, like people who had been there many times, and they were wearing various objects brought from there, which they had obtained by their services, like the Indians I had previously met. I said to them that it was not possible that the houses should be in the manner which they described to me, so to make me understand they took earth and ashes and mixed them with water, and showed how the stone is placed and the edifice reared, placing stone and mortar till the required height is reached. I asked them if the men of that country had wings to climb those stories; they laughed and explained to me a ladder as well as I could do, and they took a stick and placed it over their heads and said it was that height from story to story. Here I was also given an account of the woolen cloth of Totonteac, where they say the houses are like those at Cibola, but better and bigger, and that it is

a very great place and has no limit.

(12)   Here I learned that the coast turns to the west, almost at a right angle, because until I reached the entrance of the first desert which I passed, the coast always trended toward the north. As it was very important to know the direction of the coast, I wished to assure myself and so went to look out and I saw clearly that in latitude 35 degrees it turns to the west. I was not less pleased at this discovery than at the good news I had of the country.

(13)   So I turned to follow my route and was in that valley five days. It is so thickly populated with fine people and so provided with food that there would be enough to supply more than three hundred horse. It is all watered and is like a garden. There are villages at every half or quarter league or so. In each of them I had a very long account of Cibola, and they spoke to me in detail about it, as people would who went there each year to earn their living. Here I found a man who was a native of Cibola. He told me he had fled from the governor whom the lord had placed there in Cibola—for the lord of these seven cities lives and has his residence in one of them, which is called Ahacus, and in the others he has placed persons who command for him. This citizen of Cibola is a man of good disposition, somewhat old and much more intelligent than the natives of the valley and those I had formerly met; he told me that he wished to go with me so that I might procure his pardon. I interrogated him carefully and he told me that Cibola is a big city, that it has a large population and many streets and squares, and that in some parts of the city there are very great houses, ten stories high, in which the chiefs meet on certain days of the year. He corroborated what I had already been told, that the houses are constructed of stone and lime, and he said that the doors and fronts of the principal houses are of turquoise; he added that the others of the seven cities are similar, though some are bigger, and that the most important is Ahacus. He told me that towards the southeast lay a kingdom called Marata, in which

there used to be many very large towns, having the same kind of houses built of stone and with several stories; that this kingdom had been, and still was, at war with the lord of the seven cities; that by this war Marata had been greatly reduced in power, although it was still independent and continued the war.

(14) He likewise told me that to the southeast there is a kingdom named Totonteac, which he said was the biggest, most populous, and the richest in the world, and that there they wore clothes made of the same stuff as mine, and others of a more delicate material obtained from the animals of which I had already had a description; the people were highly cultured and different from those I had hitherto seen. He further informed me that there is another province and very great kingdom, which is called Acus—for there are Ahacus and Acus; Ahacus, with the aspiration, is one of the seven cities, the most important one, and Acus, without the aspiration, is a kingdom and province by itself.

(15) He corroborated what I had been told concerning the clothes worn in Cibola and added that all the people of that city sleep in beds raised above the floor, with fabrics and with tilts above to cover the beds. He said that he would go with me to Cibola and beyond, if I desired to take him along. I was given the same account in this town by many other persons, though not in such great detail.

(16) I traveled in this valley three days and the natives made for me all the feasts and rejoicings that they could. Here in this valley I saw more than two thousand oxhides, extremely well cured; I saw a very large quantity of turquoises and necklaces thereof, as in the places I had left behind, and all said that they came from the city of Cibola. They know this place as well as I would know what I hold in my hands, and they are similarly acquainted with the kingdoms of Marata, Acus and Totonteac. Here in this valley they brought to me a skin, half as big again as that of a large cow, and told me that it was from an animal which has only one horn on its

forehead and that this horn is curved towards its chest and then there sticks out a straight point, in which they said there was so much strength, that no object, no matter how hard, could fail to break when struck with it. They averred that there were many of these animals in that country. The color of the skin is like that of the goat and the hair is as long as one's finger.

(17)   Here I had messengers from Estéban, who told me on his behalf that he was then entering the last desert, and the more cheerfully, as he was going more assured of the country; and he sent to me to say that, since departing from me, he had never found the Indians out in any lie, but up to that point had found everything as they had told him and so he thought to find that beyond. And so I held it for certain, because it is true, that from the first day I had news of the city of Cibola, the Indians had told me of everything that till then I had seen, telling me always what towns I would find along the road and the numbers of them and, in the parts where there was no population, showing me where I would eat and sleep, without erring in one point. I had then marched, from the first place where I had news of the country, one hundred and twelve leagues, so it appears to me not unworthy to note the great truthfulness of these people. Here in this valley, as in the other towns before, I erected crosses and performed the appropriate acts and ceremonies, according to my instructions. The natives of this town asked me to stay with them three or four days, because there was a desert four leagues thence, and from the beginning of it to the city of Cibola would be a march of fifteen days and they wished to put up food for me and to make the necessary arrangements for it. They told me that with the negro Estéban there had gone more than three hundred men to accompany him and carry food, and that many wished to go with me also, to serve me and because they expected to return rich. I acknowledged their kindness and asked that they should get ready speedily, because each day seemed to me a year, so much I desired to see Cibola. And

so I remained three days without going forward, during which I continually informed myself concerning Cibola and all the other places. In doing so I took the Indians aside and questioned each one by himself, and all agreed in their account and told me the number of the people, the order of the streets, the size of the houses and the fashion of the doorways, just as I had been told by those before.

(18)   After the three days were past, many people assembled to go with me, of whom I chose thirty chiefs, who were very well supplied with necklaces of turquoises, some of them wearing as many as five or six strings. With these I took the retinue necessary to carry food for them and me and started on my way. I entered the desert on the ninth day of May. On the first day, by a very wide and well traveled road, we arrived for dinner at a place where there was water, which the Indians showed to me, and in the evening we came again to water, and there I found a shelter which the Indians had just constructed for me and another which had been made for Estéban to sleep in when he passed. There were some old huts and many signs of fire, made by people passing to Cibola over this road. In this fashion I journeyed twelve days, always very well supplied with victuals of venison, hares, and partridges of the same color and flavor as those of Spain, although rather smaller.

(19)   At this juncture I met an Indian, the son of one of the chiefs who were journeying with me, who had gone in company with the negro Estéban. This man showed fatigue in his countenance, had his body covered with sweat, and manifested the deepest sadness in his whole person. He told me that, at a day's march before coming to Cibola, Estéban, according to his custom, sent ahead messengers with his calabash, that they might know he was coming. The calabash was adorned with some rows of rattles and two feathers, one white and one red. When they arrived at Cibola, before the person of the lord's representative in that place, and gave him the calabash, as soon as he took it in his hands and saw the

rattles, with great anger he flung it on the ground and told the messengers to be gone forthwith, that he knew what sort of people these were, and that the messengers should tell them not to enter the city, as if they did so he would put them to death. The messengers went back, told Estéban what had passed. He said to them that that was nothing, that those who showed themselves irritated received him the better. So he continued his journey till he arrived at the city of Cibola, where he found people who would not consent to let him enter, who put him in a big house which was outside the city, and who at once took away from him all that he carried, his articles of barter and the turquoises and other things which he had received on the road from the Indians. They left him that night without giving anything to eat or drink either to him or to those that were with him. The following morning my informant was thirsty and went out of the house to drink from a nearby stream. When he had been there a few moments he saw Estéban fleeing away, pursued by the people of the city and they killed some of those who were with him. When this Indian saw this he concealed himself and made his way up the stream, then crossed over and regained the road of the desert. (20) At these tidings, some of the Indians who were with me commenced to weep. As for myself, the wretched news made me fear I should be lost. I feared not so much to lose my life as not to be able to return to give a report of the greatness of the country, where God, Our Lord, might be so well served and his holy faith exalted and the royal domains of H. M. extended. In these circumstances I consoled them as best I could and told them that one ought not to give entire credence to that Indian, but they said to me with many tears that the Indian only related what he had seen. So I drew apart from the Indians to commend myself to Our Lord and to pray Him to guide this matter as He might best be served and to enlighten my mind. This done, I returned to the Indians and, with a knife, cut the cords of the packages of dry goods and articles of barter which I was carrying with me and which

The Seven Cities

till then I had not touched nor given away any of the contents. I divided up the goods among all those chiefs and told them not to fear and to go along with me, which they did.

(21)   Continuing our journey, at a day's march from Cibola, we met two other Indians, of those who had gone with Estéban, who appeared bloody and with many wounds. At this meeting, they and those that were with me set up such a crying, that out of pity and fear they also made me cry. So great was the noise that I could not ask about Estéban nor of what had happened to them, so I begged them to be quiet that we might learn what had passed. They said to me: "How can we be quiet, when we know that our fathers, sons, and brothers who were with Estéban, to the number of more than three hundred men, are dead? And we no more dare go to Cibola, as we have been accustomed." Nevertheless, as well as I could, I endeavored to pacify them and to put off their fear, although I myself was not without need of someone to calm me. I asked the wounded Indians concerning Estéban and as to what had happened. They remained a short time without speaking a word, weeping along with those of their towns. At last they told me that when Estéban arrived at a day's journey from Cibola, he sent his messengers with his calabash to the lord of Cibola to announce his arrival and that he was coming peacefully and to cure them. When the messengers gave him the calabash and he saw the rattles, he flung it furiously on the floor and said: "I know these people; these rattles are not of our style of workmanship; tell them to go back immediately or not a man of them will remain alive." Thus he remained very angry. The messengers went back sad, and hardly dared to tell Estéban of the reception they had met. Nevertheless they told him and he said that they should not fear, that he desired to go on, because, although they answered him badly, they would receive him well. So he went and arrived at the city of Cibola just before sunset, with all his company, which would be more than three hundred men, besides many women. The inhabitants would not permit them to enter the city, but

put them in a large and commodious house outside the city. They at once took away from Estéban all that he carried, telling him that the lord so ordered. "All that night," said the Indians, "they gave us nothing to eat nor drink. The next day, when the sun was a lance-length high, Estéban went out of the house and some of the chiefs with him. Straightway many people came out of the city and, as soon as he saw them, he began to flee and we with him. Then they gave us these arrow-strokes and cuts and we fell and some dead men fell on top of us. Thus we lay till nightfall, without daring to stir. We heard loud voices in the city and we saw many men and women watching on the terraces. We saw no more of Estéban and we concluded that they had shot him with arrows as they had the rest that were with him, of whom there escaped only us."

(22) In view of what the Indians had related and the bad outlook for continuing my journey as I desired, I could not help but feel their loss and mine. God is witness of how much I desired to have someone of whom I could take counsel, for I confess I was at a loss what to do. I told them that Our Lord would chastize Cibola and that when the Emperor knew what had happened he would send many Christians to punish its people. They did not believe me, because they say that no one can withstand the power of Cibola. I begged them to be comforted and not to weep and consoled them with the best words I could muster, which would be too long to set down here. With this I left them and withdrew a stone's throw or two apart, to commend myself to God, and remained thus an hour and a half. When I went back to them, I found one of my Indians, named Mark, who had come from Mexico, and he said to me: "Father, these men have plotted to kill you, because they say that on account of you and Estéban their kinsfolk have been murdered, and that there will not remain a man or woman among them all who will not be killed." I then divided among them all that remained of dry stuffs and other articles, in order to pacify them. I told them to observe that if they killed me they would do me no harm, because I would die a

The Seven Cities

Christian and would go to heaven, and that those who killed me would suffer for it, because the Christians would come in search of me, and, against my will, would kill them all. With these and many other words I pacified them somewhat, although there was still high feeling on account of the people killed. I asked that some of them should go to Cibola, to see if any other Indian had escaped and to obtain some news of Estéban, but I could not persuade them to do so. Seeing this, I told them that, in any case, I must see the city of Cibola, and they said that no one would go with me. Finally, seeing me determined, two chiefs said that they would go with me.

(23)   With these and with my own Indians and interpreters, I continued my journey till I came within sight of Cibola. It is situated on a level stretch on the brow of a roundish hill. It appears to be a very beautiful city, the best that I have seen in these parts; the houses are of the type that the Indians described to me, all of stone, with their stories and terraces, as it appeared to me from a hill whence I could see it. The town is bigger than the city of Mexico. At times I was tempted to go to it, because I knew that I risked nothing but my life, which I had offered to God the day I commenced the journey; finally I feared to do so, considering my danger and that if I died, I would not be able to give an account of this country, which seems to me to be the greatest and best of the discoveries. When I said to the chiefs who were with me, how beautiful Cibola appeared to me, they told me that it was the least of the seven cities, and that Totonteac is much bigger and better than all the seven, and that it has so many houses and people that there is no end to it. Viewing the situation of the city, it occurred to me to call that country the new kingdom of St. Francis, and there, with the aid of the Indians, I made a big heap of stones and on top of it I placed a small slender cross, not having the materials to construct a bigger one. I declared that I placed that cross and landmark in the name of Don Antonio de Mendoza, viceroy and governor of New Spain and the Emperor, our lord, in sign of possession, in conformity

with my instructions. I declared that I took possession there of all the seven cities and of the kingdoms of Totonteac and Acus and Marata, and that I did not go to them, in order that I might return to give an account of what I had done and seen. (24) Then I started back, with much more fear than food, and went to meet the people whom I had left behind, with the greatest haste I could make. I overtook them after two days' march and went with them till we had passed the desert and arrived at their home. Here I was not made welcome, as previously, because the men, as well as the women, indulged in much weeping for the persons killed at Cibola. Without tarrying, I hastened in fear from that people and that valley. The first day I went ten leagues, then I went eight and again ten leagues, without stopping till I had passed the second desert. (25) On my return, although I was not without fear, I determined to approach the open tract, situated at the end of the mountain ranges, of which I said above that I had some account. As I came near, I was informed that it is peopled for many days' journey towards the east, but I dared not enter it, because it seemed to me that we must go to colonize and to rule that other country of the seven cities and the kingdoms I have spoken of, and that then one could see it better. So I forbore to risk my person and left it alone to give an account of what I had seen. However, I saw from the mouth of the [valley] seven moderate-sized towns at some distance, and further a very fresh valley of very good land, whence rose much smoke. I was informed that there is much gold in it and that the natives of it deal in vessels and jewels for the ears and little plates with which they scrape themselves to relieve themselves of sweat, and that these people will not consent to trade with those of the other part of the valley; but I was not able to learn the cause for this. Here I placed two crosses and took possession of all this plain and valley in the same manner as I had done with the other possessions, according to my instructions. From there I continued my return journey, with all the haste I could, till I arrived at the town of San Miguel, in the province of Culiacán, expecting to find there Francisco Vázquez de Coronado, governor of New Galicia. As I did not find him there, I continued my journey to the city of Compostella, where I found him. From there I immediately wrote word of my coming to the most illustrious lord, the viceroy of New Spain, and to our father provincial, Friar Antonio, of Ciudad-Rodrigo, asking him to send me orders what to do.

(26)   I omit here many particulars which are not pertinent; I simply tell what I saw and what was told me concerning the countries where I went and those of which I was given information, in order to make a report to our father provincial, that he may show it to the father of our order, who may advise him, or to the council of the order, at whose command I went, that they may give it to the most illustrious lord, the viceroy of New Spain, at whose request they sent me on the journey.

———————◄●►———————

Now as simple and as straightforward as this document seems to be, it has been a bone of contention for centuries. Does it have the "ring of truth" about it as some have said? Or are the important points mere fabrications—is it in fact a tissue of lies as most have judged it? If Fray Marcos was lying then he began to lie in a very big way right from the beginning. He could not have intended merely to color the truth slightly, for not only did he make these statements frankly and openly, he made them repeatedly; and there is no hint whatever of that judicious, ponderous wording which tends to imply more than is actually said.

Before returning to Mexico to witness the consequences of this report it might be well to pause briefly and examine the strange reaction of the lord of Cibola to Estéban's decorated gourd. It came as a surprise since one would not normally expect a powerful ruler to be so merciless toward a small, unarmed group who clearly meant him no harm. We find a hint in the word rendered "rattle" in the above translation; it is *cascabel* in the original, and it signifies a bell having a clapper trapped within an enclosure. The common sleigh bell is a good example, and because of the similarity in construction the same word is used to signify the rattles of a rattlesnake. Now what kind of cascabells did Estéban have on his gourd? If they were snake rattles then there is no obvious way to understand the Cibolan's violent reaction to them. But there were certain Aztec artisans in the vicinity of Mexico City who produced genuine cascabells of copper, silver, and also of gold by the sophisticated "lost wax" casting process [18]. Numerous examples of such bells have been found, even well into the present territory of the United States.

If these were the rattles which Estéban had attached to his calabash then they would have betrayed his origin. A few words of explanation from the messengers describing the foreigner who owned that gourd might well have been enough to excite the Cibolan into a fury. For nearly twenty years had passed since the foreign conquerers had taken Mexico, and to be realistic one must imagine that at least the rulers at Cibola were aware of the fate of the Aztec nation. They might have looked upon Estéban, then, as the scout for an army which would later come against them as well, which, of course, he was.

Chapter 2:

EXPEDITION OF CONQUEST

WHEN THE FRIAR returned to Mexico with such glowing accounts of those marvelous cities it was only a matter of days before an army of volunteers began to assemble, eager to undertake an expedition of conquest. Francisco Vázquez de Coronado, the Governor of New Galicia, was appointed Captain General. He was a man of barely twenty-nine years at the time, but this meteoric rise was not due entirely to his skill as executive or strategist; other factors weighed heavily as well. Usually, as we shall see again, operations of this kind were privately financed, and the expedition to Cibola was no exception. It was a joint venture, paid for partly by the Viceroy out of his own pocket and partly by Coronado himself—and perhaps by his wife who was wealthy in her own right. The backers expected their rewards, then, from the wealth which they hoped would be taken, and a certain portion was claimed by the King as well.

It was agreed that the volunteers should rendezvous on Shrove Tuesday (1540) at Compostella, the Capital City of New Galicia, and then and there begin their march for Cibola. Fray Marcos, having been promoted to the rank of Father Provincial, was to go along—as chaplain at least, but whether as guide remains to be seen. On the appointed day Mendoza himself harangued the assembled troops to encourage them on their way; and then, with colors flying, they were off! In keeping with the festive atmosphere, the Viceroy accompanied the army for the first two days of march, and then he returned to Mexico City.

The little army was a motley troop consisting of some 330 Spaniards, 1000 friendly Indians, and a few Negros. They were equipped with about a thousand horses which carried the provisions, and they also took some livestock on the hoof to be used for food along the way. Three ships laden with additional supplies were dispatched up the western coast to support the effort if a rendezvous could be effected. Only a few of the Spaniards were professional, experienced soldiers. The majority were young men of elite families who had come to the New World in search of their fortunes and were not gainfully employed at the time. This is how it happened that the group sprang into being so quickly. They needed only the word. Many others were eager to go but a strict limit was imposed on the numbers of both Spaniards and Indians in order that the security of the new colony should not be compromised. When one considers the situation thoughtfully, he must surely marvel that this small, unproven force should have had the daring to undertake an expedition of this kind against cities as great as Fray Marcos had described—cities, moreover, which lay so very far away. The Spaniards had superior weapons, to be sure, but their fire-power was sorely limited so they would have no hope whatever against that multitude if the Cibolans should resist valiantly.

The army rested for a time at Culiacán, the last Spanish outpost along the way, where they took advantage of the opportunity to replenish their supplies. But there Coronado modified the order of march somewhat. Instead of moving ahead as a unit he decided to proceed with a smaller, more manageable detachment of fifty horsemen, a small infantry, Fray Marcos, and a few Indians and Negros; the rest of the troops were to follow along behind in two weeks. This arranged, the General and that advance portion of the army set out into the wilderness beyond. But did they follow the same route which Fray Marcos had explored previously?

With hardly any exceptions, historians have shared the firm belief that Coronado did accurately retrace that former course. After all, why would he not? Marcos was present to point the way, and the unattractive alternative would have been to strike out blindly into an uncharted wilderness trusting in luck alone to lead him to his destination. But since the pueblos that he finally conquered were not great cities such as the Friar had described one has grounds for suspecting that he deviated somewhere along the way. Accordingly, instead of merely assuming that the routes were the same, let us try to determine the truth for ourselves. To this end we consult the only other prime source of information which is known to exist, namely, the report that Coronado himself wrote to the Viceroy on August 3, 1540 after he had successfully taken those seven small towns. Let us read a few paragraphs of it. He begins by describing the laborious journey northwards from Culiacán in these words [5;p.280]:

> On the 22nd of April last, I set out from the province of Culiacán with a part of the army. Judging by the outcome, it was fortunate that I did not take the whole of the army with me on this undertaking. The labors have been so very great and the lack of food such that I do not believe this undertaking could have been completed before the end of this year, and not without a great loss of life.
>
> Thirty leagues before reaching the place of which the father provincial, Fray Marcos, spoke so well in his report— the valley into which Fray Marcos did not dare enter—I sent Melchior Diaz forward with fifteen horsemen, ordering him to make but one day's journey out of two, so that he could examine everything there before I arrived. He traveled through some very rough mountains for four days, and did not find anything to live on, or people, or information about anything except two or three poor villages. From the people there he learned that there was nothing to be found in the country beyond except the mountains, which continued very

rough, entirely uninhabited by people. The whole company felt disturbed at this, that a thing so much praised, and about which the father had said so many things, should be found so very different; and they began to think that all the rest would be of the same sort...

He has only just begun, but it is already clear that something is amiss for note that he found the terrain "very different" from what Marcos had described in his report. But let us keep the central problem uppermost in our minds, that is, we must decide whether the Friar described the terrain inaccurately as Coronado charged, or whether in fact he described different terrain altogether. As his report continues, the General makes frequent reference to a "Valley of Hearts", and that merits a brief explanation in advance.

Recall that some four years prior to this expedition the Cabeza de Vaca party had passed through that same mountainous area. At one village along the way the four were feasted lavishly and were offered the dried hearts of 600 deer, so they called the place "Hearts" in memory of the occasion. The village was situated in the mountainous region, but shortly after quitting it they negotiated a pass and emerged into the coastal lowlands. Most modern authorities think that village was near the present town of Ures (see Figure 1) and that they continued from there down along the valley of the Sonora River. Its actual location is of no real concern to us here, but it is interesting and significant that Coronado should have thought to locate himself in that valley.

For let us recall further that Marcos made no mention of the Valley of Hearts in his narrative, and how would he ever have identified it in any case? Estéban might have pointed it out if they actually had passed through, but of course he and Marcos parted company very early along the way so that would not have been possible. How, then, did Coronado identify the valley? One might guess that they met natives who remembered the four from that previous occasion, but note in what follows that the General states he "reached the Valley of Hearts, *at last,* ...", suggesting that it was no mere chance encounter but a planned goal. This question constitutes a little mystery all of its own, but a plausible solution should suggest itself to the reader by the time we finish this discussion. Let us now return to that report and read a few more paragraphs.

I reached the Valley of Hearts, at last, on the 26th of May, and rested there a number of days. Between Culiacán and this place I could sustain myself only by means of a large supply of corn bread, because I had to leave all the corn, as it was not yet ripe. In this Valley of Hearts, we found more people than in any part of the country we had left behind, and a large extent of tilled ground. There was no corn for food among them, but I heard that there was some in another valley called Sonora. As I did not wish to disturb them by force, I sent Melchior Diaz, with goods to exchange for it. A little corn was obtained by trading, which relieved the friendly Indians and some Spaniards.

Ten or twelve of the horses had died of overwork by the time we reached this Valley of Hearts, because they were unable to stand the strain of carrying heavy burdens and eating so little. Some of our Negros and some of the Indians also died here, which was a great loss for the rest of the expedition. They told me that the Valley of Hearts is a long five days' journey from the western sea. I sent to summon Indians from the coast in order to learn about their condition, and while I was waiting for these, the horses rested. I stayed there four days, during which the Indians came from the sea...

I set out from Hearts and kept near the seacoast as well as I could judge. But I found myself continually farther off, so that when I reached Chichilticale I found I was fifteen days' journey from the sea, although the father provincial said it was only five leagues distant and that he had seen it. We all became very distrustful, and felt great anxiety and dismay to see that everything was the reverse of what he had told Your Lordship. The sea turns toward the west directly opposite the Hearts for ten or twelve leagues. There I learned that the ships had been seen which Your Lordship had sent in search of the port of Chichilticale, which Fray Marcos had said was on the thirty-fifth degree.

These few paragraphs tell us all we need to know for the present, so let us note the significant points in turn. Recall that in Paragraph 5 of his account Fray Marcos stated that he was writing down the names of the villages on another piece of paper. That piece of paper did not survive the years, and the name Chichilticale does not appear in his narrative; but we know from what Coronado has just written that it was a village near the sea at a point where the coastline turns sharply to the west. Judging from this part of the description it must have been located near the site of the present city of Guaymas, but in that case it would have been close to 28 degrees, not 35 as Marcos reported.

This is a fairly large discrepancy in latitude, but the only alternative would be to look for this village somewhere near the northern end of the Gulf where the coast makes another sharp turn to the west. At about 31 degrees, that would be closer to the figure Marcos specified, but the terrain itself argues against this idea. For Fray Marcos stated that the town he visited had an expanse of green fields around it; namely, there was arable farm land and the water to sustain it. We find both of these resources in the vicinity of Guaymas, but not at the northern end of the Gulf. In actual fact, the thirty-fifth parallel passes over 200 miles north of the extreme end of the Gulf so the Friar was greatly in error with respect to the latitude in any case. Evidently one must conclude that he did not have instruments at hand for making the measurement accurately.

Now the second thing that we learn from Coronado's

report is that this was the place where that rendezvous with the supply ships was supposed to take place. Without a doubt, then, the plan was to stay near the coast so they could pass through that village. This simple conclusion is confirmed by Coronado himself, for he states explicitly that he tried to follow the coast but failed in the attempt and found himself continually further from the sea as he advanced along a northerly course.

And then, finally, we learn that although the General never reached the coast to rendezvous with the supply ships, he arrived at Chichilticale nevertheless—but it proved to be fifteen days' journey inland from the sea, not one day's march as Marcos had described it. What an implausible error this is! And we find that it becomes even more implausible upon closer examination: Many years afterwards one of the soldiers in that army, Pedro de Castañeda by name, was encouraged to write his recollections of the expedition, and here is how that chronicler remembered the episode at Chichilticale [36;p. 313]:

> When the general had passed through all the inhabited region to Chichilticale, where the desert begins, and saw that there was nothing good, he could not repress his sadness, notwithstanding the marvels that were promised further on. No one save the Indians who accompanied the negro had seen them* and already on many occasions they had been caught in lies. He was especially afflicted to find this Chichilticale, of which so much had been boasted, to be a single, ruined and roofless house, which at one time seemed to have been fortified. It was easy to see that this house, which was built of red earth, was the work of civilized people who had come from afar.

---

* *The implied accusation is that upon hearing of Estéban's fate, Fray Marcos had immediately turned and hastened homeward in fright, writing in his report what the Indians had told him about Cibola and inventing the rest.*

THE LOST CITIES OF CIBOLA

So the coastal village of Chichilticale which Coronado expected to find, at which the rendezvous with his supply ships was supposed to take place, turned out to be a single mud house, standing in ruins, fifteen days' journey inland from the sea! What followed is anticlimactic, but let us continue along and note how the expedition ended nevertheless. Leaving that old mud house behind the army pressed northward, and after fifteen days they spied "Cibola". Here is how Castañeda described it:

> On the following day, in good order, we entered the inhabited country. Cibola was the first village we discovered; on beholding it the army broke forth with maledictions on Friar Marcos de Niza. God grant that he may feel none of them.
>
> Cibola is built on a rock; this village is so small that, in truth, there are many farms in New Spain that make a better appearance. It may contain two hundred warriors...

Here was bitter disappointment indeed, a sorry prize to have been gained at such a cost. But why would Fray Marcos have been so brash as to have identified those little pueblos as Cibola inasmuch as they disagreed in every possible particular with the description he had already sworn to? Did the inhabitants themselves call their villages Cibola? Coronado gives the answer to this question himself as he continues his report.

> It now remains to tell about this city and kingdom and province of which the father provincial gave Your Lordship an account. In brief, I can assure you that he has not told the truth in a single thing that he said, except the name of the city and the large stone houses. Although they are not decorated with turquoises nor made of lime or of good bricks, nevertheless they are very good houses with three and four and five stories, very good apartments and rooms with corridors. There some very good rooms under ground and paved, which are made for winter, and are something like hot baths. The ladders which they have

for their houses are all moveable and portable.

The Seven Cities are seven little villages, all having the kind of houses I have described. They are all within a radius of five leagues. Each has its own name and no single one is called Cibola, but altogether are called Cibola...

And thus ends the story of the Seven Cities of Cibola as History has preserved it these four hundred and forty-five years. It's a tale marred by such obvious falsehood that one must be watchful if he is not to be deceived. Accordingly, it might be well to ask of those little villages: By whom were they called Cibola? Not by the natives, surely, for they called themselves Zuni, and they continue to do so to this very day.

Now we started out to determine if Coronado followed the same path northward that Marcos had explored earlier, and we have come part way. At least it is obvious that he did not follow the route outlined in the narrative, for without a doubt the army stayed well inland from the sea while Marcos explicitly described a route near the coast. Even so, Coronado claimed to have retraced the Friar's tested path and to have arrived successfully at Chichilticale and then finally at Cibola. His charge was that the priest had lied about the terrain in his report and had exaggerated many important details. Of course it's quite clear that someone took great liberties with the truth, but if Marcos was the culprit then he could have lied either about his first trip or the second. That is, he might have intentionally led the army into entirely different territory than he had covered before, but if that were the case the General did not seem to suspect, because he did not accuse Marcos of having directed him along the wrong route, either deliberately or otherwise.

Many generations of historians have taken Coronado at his word and have judged the Friar's detailed narrative to be a tissue of lies. Cowardice is given as the motive. Upon hearing of Estéban's fate Marcos supposedly feared for his own life, gave up all thought of proceeding to Cibola, and promptly turned his feet homeward. But while this might give him reason for lying about events mentioned after he heard of the massacre, it does not suggest why he would have lied about those many inconsequential details which came before. In particular, there is no obvious reason why fear of proceeding to Cibola should have caused him to lie about the route he followed beforehand or the villages he visited along the way. Long established custom decrees that the accuser should bear the burden of proof, but we have seen no proof at all. Since Coronado never examined those coastal regions his charges against the Friar's narrative have no visible foundation, so why should our critical attention not be turned to the General himself instead?

It's easy to imagine that the army, burdened as it was with armament and pack horses, simply may not have been able to proceed along the exact route Marcos pointed out. The General may have been obliged to seek a detour, and, as things worked out, he continually found himself cut off from the coast by impassable mountains. This seems sound enough, but such factors could have been openly acknowledged in his report; there would have been no call whatever to impugn the priest's word or suggest that he was at fault in any way. As an alternative, one might suppose that Coronado recklessly disregarded his guide's direction, and, in his impatience, sought a more direct route northward. Later on, fearing the Viceroy's censure because of the outcome, he decided to claim that Marcos had actually led him along that inland course. It would be his word against the Friar's.

If one examines his letter to the Viceroy again with this possibility in mind, then he might easily conclude that Coronado had already decided to forsake the coastal route by the time he left that last outpost at Culiacán. One could then understand why he divided the army into those two groups. Presumably he was preparing for rough going even though the Friar had spoken of easy terrain ahead in his narrative. In fact, according to Sauer [35;p.10], there are no more than isolated hills in the region south of Guaymas along the coast so they probably could have followed that route as a unit without difficulty just as the narrative had promised. But the General seems to have known even before testing it that the terrain was going to be more severe than was described in that earlier report, and this gives reason to suspect that he might have been the one after all who led the way northward out of Culiacán—and along a deliberately alternate route.

Although no doubt unintentionally, he provided a measure of support for this view in his own report, for recall the statement: "I ... kept near the seacoast as well as I could judge. But I found myself continually farther off, ...". He gave no hint here that he was yielding to another's direction; in fact, he could hardly have stated more clearly that the judgement of route was his own. Moreover, it is easy to see that he was not retracing a course which had been explored in advance—one whose destination was already known.

So one can find at least a hint of evidence to support that unsavory idea, but what an implausible picture it brings to mind. On the one hand is the suggestion of a mendacious priest who either wantonly lied, or who betrayed his trust and led the expedition astray into unexplored wilderness. And now on the other hand is an alternative equally as unrealistic. One must imagine a gentleman of honor, the general of an army, who lied to his commander in order to place the blame for his own blunders upon the shoulders of another—and of one whom he accepted as a man of God at that! Surely it is necessary to look somewhere else for understanding.

And perhaps it can be found by recalling that the expedition to Cibola was organized very quickly. Stimulated by a frantic lust for great riches, it mushroomed into being almost overnight. Coronado himself was overcome with the fever of anticipation, and he concentrated his own energies upon the growing enterprise. It was an enormous task; there was much work to be done, so there was no time to lose if they were to be ready to leave by spring.

Accordingly it was not until the expedition was well underway, perhaps during their journey between Compostella and Culiacán, that Coronado and Marcos would have had a chance to speak at length about those great cities which they had set out to conquer. The Friar would then have described in detail their unending expanse, their countless warriors, and the vast, barren desert which surrounded and protected them. That would have given Coronado his first sound basis for realistically assessing the outcome of their venture, and he must then have realized that his little army was marching to its certain doom! Presumably Marcos had anticipated that a force worthy of the objective would have been recruited. But when he observed the small group which had actually assembled he clearly saw the futility of the enterprise, and he must have persuaded Coronado of that grim reality.

But what was to be done about it? The General could hardly turn back at that point; he would have been branded for life. Honor required that he press forward—but he need not have pressed forward along the correct road! Perhaps Coronado reasoned that it would be better to explore an entirely new territory, hoping to find wealth as yet unknown, than to persist along the road to certain death for all. But here let us insert that key condition mentioned earlier and insist that despite the outward appearances he acted both honorably and sensibly as befitted a man of his station. Then the fact that he accused Marcos of lying rather than of being lost *requires that they were partners in the plan.* Being a gentleman, the General would never have devised such a tactic, and neither would he have been so foolish as to expect his charges to stand if the Friar should have chosen to defend himself. The only plausible resolution of this seemingly incongruous situation, then, is that Marcos *offered* to play the role of liar so the army would not need to go against

Cibola and be destroyed. It would be one man's reputation in return for the lives of thirteen hundred.

Presumably, then, the army marched into the wilderness with the Friar pretending to lead the way, but both he and the General knew full well that they would never arrive at their avowed destination. It must have been Marcos after all who identified that old mud house as Chichilticale and the Zuni pueblos as Cibola. So the report was written, the charges were made, and Fray Marcos de Niza was dispatched back to Mexico in disgrace along with the messenger who carried the report. He would not dispute the accusations; on the contrary, he would meekly confess to them and spend the rest of his days in ignomy—an object of reproach to his brethren. One can easily imagine that their parting on that sad occasion would have been a sober and moving experience for both men.

So here at last is a realistic interpretation of the events which not only squares with the records, it also accounts for the discrepancies between them. And even more significantly, it casts men in roles that they could have played in good conscience. They were rational human beings, true to their creeds, who behaved responsibly, fearlessly and honorably* at every turn; judged by the lights of their time, neither bears any stigma whatever. Did Coronado betray a trust by departing from the prearranged course? As commander in the field, having the more accurate information, his was the final responsibility, and he exercised it both prudently and wisely. There was at least hope of reward somewhere along that alternate route, but there was none at all at Cibola. So it was the only responsible course, but had he made it openly he could never have defended himself against the inevitable charge of cowardice from his detractors. He would not risk that whatever the cost.

---

* *It seems obvious that the propriety of their behavior (as far as we are concerned in this context) can only be judged in light of the customs of their own social order.*

Likewise we now see Fray Marcos in an honorable role that is accurately true to life. It's not easy to sympathize with his yearning to propagate his faith through armed conquest, but that was the custom of the day. However, when the cause was doomed to failure, he must have felt the blood of those 1300 on his own hands since he had been instrumental in bringing the effort about. His offering to be the lamb, then, is realistic, and, as an act of atonement, also honorable and even heroic. How much more plausible he is playing this part than that of a foolish, lying priest who betrayed a solomn trust with no extenuating motive whatever! Truly, disciplined men do not change their stripes easily.

Where, then, was Cibola? If we wish to find those Seven Cities then we must ignore all the analyses which have gone before and take our lead from the one man who was there and returned to tell of it. Much scholarly argument would have been avoided if Fray Marcos had been more explicit with some of the details, but nevertheless his narrative defines the way very well. Only two legs of the trek remain after that singular point where the coastline turns sharply to the west so we can hardly go far astray if we join him there in Paragraph 12. In the next paragraph Marcos states that he was in "that valley for five days", and here the first problem arises for he does not say how far he was from that starting point on the coast when he made the statement. We have to guess.

It seems most probable that he would have entered the note in his diary just as he was leaving "that valley", and if so then, since only five days are in question altogether, we cannot be far wrong if we guess that he was two days' travel from that notable point on the coast at the time. In all of Paragraphs 13, 14, and 15 he says nothing whatever to indicate any further progress, but then at last, in Paragraph 16, he records the passage of three more days and completes the first of those two remaining legs of the journey. Having thus traveled about five days since leaving that point near the sea where the coast turns sharply to the west he would have gained some 80 miles, and that would bring him near the site of the present city of Hermosillo on the Sonora River.

Now it is true that we had to guess at those two days, but that can hardly raise serious doubt about his position at this late stage of the journey. For reassurance, one can lean upon a principle stressed by Carl Sauer in his attempts to analyze the Fray Marcos narrative [35]. Sauer urged, in brief, that the cities of today were the villages of yesterday, and the roads of today were their trails. This seems reasonable enough since population centers develop where the land is good and where water is available for agriculture. The most immediate conclusion to be drawn from this is that the village which Marcos just left behind grew into the present city of Guaymas. Hermosillo is the next main stop along the way northward today, and it fits, being about 80 miles distant.

One can hardly be certain of the exact spot, of course, but there is no need to be precise here because the target destination is so very great. The important point is that twelve miles away began an unpopulated region which required fifteen days to cross, and that could only have been the vast Sonoran desert! One can appreciate the futility of the Coronado enterprise all the more at this point, for what would those thousand horses and thirteen hundred men have done for food and drink in that destitute wasteland?

Now Baldwin's translation misses a shade of meaning with respect to those fifteen days mentioned in Paragraph 17, a point which most other translators bring out explicitly. The original reads "..., hay *largos* quince dias de camino."— that is, a *long* fifteen days' march. Although Fray Marcos indicates that they planned to cross the unpopulated region in fifteen days, apparently more than the normal exertion would be required in order to do so. Since the terrain at hand is not especially mountainous, then presumably more than the customary 15.5 miles would be covered each day. In order to gain some idea of what this might mean, let us note how Cleve Hallenbeck analyzed the problem. One ought to be aware that this author shared the common view that Marcos traveled through the same rough country which Coronado later described. Since the terrain in the Sonoran Desert is not generally so severe, Hallenbeck's conclusions might be regarded as safely conservative [16;p.43]:

> Marcos made his journey on foot over unimproved Indian trails, and tramping the old trails of the southwest is real work. I have covered hundreds of miles of them, afoot and mounted... By the time one has traveled fifteen miles under such conditions he has done a fair day's work, although he may have covered an air-line distance of no more than a dozen miles...

The author describes the many difficulties which would have confronted those travelers along the trail, and then he concludes as follows:

> ... I know from my own observation and experience that for a tolerable pedestrian on a march of a week or more on the trails of the semiarid Southwest, even today an average of sixteen miles a day is fair going, twenty miles a very good pace, and twenty-four miles an exceptionally fast rate that I doubt could be maintained for a week under summertime conditions.

There can be no doubt that the air-line distance gained must be somewhat less than the distance covered on the ground, but the difference need not have been great because the terrain in the Sonoran Desert is not generally as rough as Hallenbeck has considered here. We must also keep in mind that Marcos followed a well-worn path, one which had been determined by years of Indian travel to be the best possible route. Therefore, since Fray Marcos and the Indians were obviously "tolerable pedestrians", well hardened to the trail, let's grant them the twenty miles per day which Hallenbeck says is a very good pace. In that case they should have covered about 300 miles in those fifteen long days.

Figure 2 illustrates the conclusions reached thus far. The Friar's approximate position in Paragraph 12, the site of the present city of Guaymas, is indicated by the letter "G". His position five days later is given by the "H", corresponding to Hermosillo. An arc of 300 miles radius has been swung about this point as center; presumably his destination was not far from this curve. The cities could hardly have been situated much to the east or the Coronado expedition would have spied them in passing. Neither could they have been located further to the west, closer to the mouth of the Colorado, since this region was examined by other parties during that same time period, and nothing was found. So there can be little doubt that if the Seven Cities ever existed at all then they must have been situated somewhere within that central region. This is an encouraging conclusion indeed because either the Gila River or the Salt River would provide enough water to support a substantial population.

Fray Marcos de Niza played his part faithfully to the end. He went to his grave on the 25th of March in 1558 without uttering another word about the matter as far as anyone knows, and he has been known to historians as the "Lying Monk" ever since. On that day the curtain fell on the first act of this great drama. The obvious question now is this: If Fray Marcos was the first, then who was the next European to enter that region, and what did he find there? Oddly enough, the entr'acte was a long one for we must wait a great many years to meet the next man with a pen who came anywhere near.

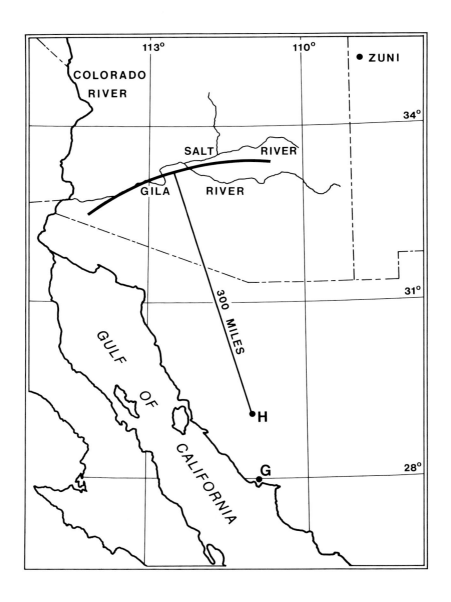

FIGURE 2

Chapter 3:

THE SEQUEL

AFTER THE ZUNI villages had been taken, Coronado cast about to see if the new land held anything of value which could redeem the expedition. He sent scouting parties east into the panhandle region of Texas and also westward as far as the Grand Canyon of the Colorado, but they found nothing of interest anywhere. Hearing reports of a rich kingdom to the northeast the General himself led a small detachment well into what is now Kansas only to find that he had been deceived by a deliberate hoax; it was the ruse of a wily Indian who tried to lure the army to its destruction. Theirs was a valiant but disappointing effort. They searched an enormous territory, but they found no riches whatever.

Then, early in the spring of 1542, the General suffered a serious head injury during practice maneuvers, and his life hung in the balance for a time. He regained his feet at last, but that former driving ambition was gone; the country was destitute and worthless, and he yearned only to return to Mexico and home. But many of the troops were strongly opposed to abandoning the newly gained territory despite its poverty, so they began the homeward trek a divided and demoralized band, their spirit and discipline badly decayed. When they had set out from Mexico two years before every man among them had been the envy of all who were left behind. Without a doubt they would each gain wealth, lands and titles and return to tell glorious tales of conquest. As it turned out they straggled home a beggarly lot with the General himself on a stretcher near the end—but they did return. Despite the Viceroy's disappointment Coronado was allowed to resume his duties as Governor of New Galicia, but he was removed after two years when his ability to manage the office became doubtful; apparently he did not fully recover from his injury. However he continued to serve as a minor public official for another decade, and he died peacefully in 1554 during his 44th year.

The dismal reports from that expedition effectively shattered the dream of riches in the north. Additional tales of Cibola which might have filtered south could only have been met with snickers of derision since no further efforts were ever made in that direction. If Coronado had reported merely that he searched the region and found no such cities then interest might have been rekindled by new and specific accounts, but, as it was, Cibola had been found and identified. The matter was settled. And such tales would likely have become less and less frequent as time went by because of the massacre of Estéban and his party. Those Indians who lived directly on the road to the great cities would be afraid to go back, as they themselves had said, and they would pass the word along to others who were going there as well. Moreover, the Cibolans themselves might have thought it prudent to bring that former traffic with the south to an end; if so they could have devised still other methods for discouraging it. In view of the circumstances, then, perhaps it's not surprising that the Seven Cities remained as they were, veiled in obscurity, while the years turned slowly into decades.

And the decades passed freely for we must wait a century and a half to meet the next European who ventured into that region. He was Eusebio Francisco Kino, a Jesuit priest and missionary originally from the Tyrolean district of Austria. Kino had no particular interest in missionary work until, as he believed, he was miraculously cured of a serious illness. After his recovery he volunteered for foreign service and requested assignment to the most dangerous of the mission fields—his first choice being the Mariannas, or, failing that, China. But he was ordered to Mexico instead, to which he embarked early in the year 1681 out of Cadiz.

Father Kino was a man of many interests, including both astronomy and mathematics, and upon arriving in the New World his first act was to see to the printing of a short monograph detailing his theories and observations of the great comet which had just recently receded. This done, he pursued his assignment to the San Bruno settlement in (Lower) California where he remained for six years. But eventually that colony had to be abandoned so he returned to Mexico to receive his next assignment as missionary to the Pimas. Their domain, Pimería Alta as it was called, comprised most of what is now Sonora and that part of Arizona which lies south of the Gila River [HEE-la]. It was bounded on the east by the land of the Apaches and on the west by the Colorado River and the Gulf of California.

Kino arrived at the frontier of settlement in 1687 and founded his first mission, Nuestra Senora de los Dolores, at a site near the present town of Magdelena, about a hundred miles north of Hermosillo. This was to be his home and headquarters for the remainder of his life, but he explored extensively to the north and northwest and established a string of missions which extended as far north as Tucson. Let us hear Bolton summarize Father Kino's accomplishments because he confirms the fact that this priest was the first white man to enter that region since the time of Fray Marcos [6;p.53]:

> Kino's work as missionary was paralleled by his achieve-
> ment as explorer, and to him is due the credit for the first
> mapping of Pimeria Alta on the basis of actual exploration.

THE LOST CITIES OF CIBOLA

The region had been entered by Fray Marcos, by Melchior Diaz, and by the main Coronado party, in the period 1539-1541. But these explorers had only passed along its eastern and western borders; for it is no longer believed that they went down the Santa Cruz. Not since that day—a century and a half before—had Arizona been entered from the south by a single recorded expedition, while, so far as we know, not since 1605, when Oñate went from Moqui down the Colorado of the West, had any white man seen the Gila River. The rediscovery, therefore, and the first interior exploration of Pimería Alta was the work of Father Kino.

During his journeys northward from the Mission Dolores, Kino continued to hear reports of deserted cities further to the north, but it was not until 1694 that he actually mounted an expedition and set out to investigate them. Here is how he described that incident in his memoirs [6;I,p.127]:

> In November, 1694, I went inland with my servants and some justices of this Pimeria, as far as the *casa grande,* as the Pimas call it, which is on the large river of [Gila] that flows out of Nuevo Mexico and has its source near Acoma...
>
> The *casa grande* is a four-story building, as large as a castle and equal to the largest church in these lands of Sonora. It is said that the ancestors of Montezuma deserted and depopulated it, and, beset by the neighboring Apaches, left for the east or *Casas Grandes**, and that from there they turned towards the south and southwest, finally founding the great city and court of Mexico. Close to this *casa grande* there are thirteen smaller houses, somewhat more dilap-idated, and the ruins of many others, which make it evident that there had been a city here. On this occasion and on later ones I have learned and heard, and at times have seen, that further to the east, north and west there are seven or eight more of these large old houses and the ruins of whole cities, with many broken *metates* and jars, charcoal, etc. These certainly must be the Seven Cities mentioned by the holy man, Fray Marcos de Niza, who in his long

* *Another site entirely, presumably in northern Mexico.*

pilgrimage came clear to the Bacapa* rancheria of these coasts, which is about sixty leagues southwest from this *casa grande,* and about twenty leagues from the Sea of California. The guides or interpreters must have given his Reverence the information which he has in his book concerning these Seven Cities, although certainly at that time, and for a long while before, they must have been deserted...

Here is the first statement of a riddle which was to become a stumbling block for many years to come because the spectacle which Father Kino gazed upon that day bore all the obvious marks of extreme antiquity. A century and a half had passed since Fray Marcos had observed those cities alive and thriving, but even that great span of time seemed wholly inadequate to account for the ruin which lay before him; Kino thought the cities must have been deserted even longer than that. And yet the picture was one of strange contradiction as closer inspection revealed: Three years later, in the year 1697, accompanied by a troop of soldiers, Father Kino made another expedition into the north, and he stopped again at this *casa grande.* He recorded the following additional details on that occasion [6;I,p.172]:

> The soldiers were much delighted to see the Casa Grande. We marveled at seeing that it was about a league from the river and without water; but afterward we saw that it had a large aqueduct with a very great embankment, which must have been three *varas*† high and six or seven wide—wider than the causeway of Guadalupe at Mexico. This very great aqueduct, as is still seen, not only conducted the water from the river to the Casa Grande, but at the

---

* *The letters B and V are all but interchangeable in the Spanish language so the names were probably the same; Father Kino merely spelled the word differently. But this must be a coincidence since Marcos passed through Vacapa very early in his trek (Paragraph 3); the site mentioned here by Kino was therefore far to the north.*
† *A* vara *is just slightly less than 33 inches.*

same time, making a great turn, it watered and enclosed a champaign many leagues in length and breadth, and of very level and very rich land. With ease, also, one could now restore and roof the house and repair the great aqueduct for a very good pueblo,...

So the great house itself was not in such a bad state of repair; at that time it would have been easy to restore the building and make it serviceable again. And even more definite testimony to this same effect can be cited, for among the soldiers escorting Father Kino on that journey was a Lieutenant Juan Mateo Manje who kept a detailed diary of his experiences. Some years later Manje wrote a book in which he told of his adventures in this new land, and there he described the events at hand as follows [21;p.85]:

> We continued to the west. After four leagues, we arrived at mid-day at *Casas Grandes**, inside of which Father Kino said mass even though he had traveled without eating until then. One of the houses was a large building four stories high with the main room in the center, with walls two *varas* in width made of strong *argamasa y barro* and so smooth inside that they looked like brushed wood and so polished that they shone like Puebla earthenware. The corners of the windows are square and very straight, without sills or wooden frames. They must have been made in a mould. The same may be said of the doors...

The word picture that he paints here calls to mind a very well preserved structure indeed; there is no suggestion whatever of erosion or decay even though the city at large lay utterly in ruins. In fact, the scene appears so incongruous that one might suspect that he overstated the case somewhat in order to heighten the sense of drama in his book. However, there still exists today an original manuscript, signed by Manje himself, in which he recounted those same events

* *Clearly, the site had not yet acquired a fixed name.*

again in slightly different words. A translation of this other document is included as a supplement in Reference 21, and the portion of interest reads as follows [21;p.287]:

> ...The walls of a strong conglomerate of dried mud, two *varas* thick, were so smooth and polished that there was not the slightest hole. Likewise the corners of the windows and doors were so straight and regular in size that they looked like they had been moulded and were smoothed to a fine finish. The natives of this vicinity had set fire to and burned the roofs, which were of a non-decaying timber...

Evidently, then, although the smaller buildings making up the rest of the city lay in ruins, this great structure was in surprisingly good condition at the time. The witness stressed this point particularly, and he said it not once but twice. Now it's important to notice that the building was made of mud so even the rain would erode it, as is evident from the photo in Plate 1 which shows the Casa Grande as it appeared at some (unspecified) time near the turn of this century, about 200 years after Manje saw it. There can be no mistaking the changes which the wind and the rain have wrought, but it seems obvious that this great degradation could not have progressed far by Manje's time or he would not have felt moved to marvel at the smooth, flawless walls and the straight doors and windows. It is true that Manje spoke especially of the inside walls in the passage quoted from his book, but he also mentioned the doors and windows as being in similarly very good condition. And, since the roof had been burned, even the inside walls were exposed to the weather by the time he saw them. In order for the building to have been in such fine condition, then, one would think that it must have been in use and actively maintained until only a very short time before the Lieutenant came upon the scene—a time short, that is, compared to two hundred years.

PLATE 1: *The Casa Grande ruin as it appeared around 1900. Reproduced from an undated print in the Arizona Historical Foundation collection at the Arizona State University Library.*

The Sequel

PLATE 2: *The Casa Grande as it remains today, a National Monument near Coolidge, Arizona.*

The Casa Grande is now preserved as a National Monument, and Plate 2 shows the structure as it is today. Some of the damage has been repaired around the base, and a roof has been erected to protect it from further damage from the rain; nothing remains of the rest of the ancient city.

Continuing with his account of that expedition into the unknown lands, Manje goes on to describe an interesting site just downstream from this Casa Grande. His narrative continues as follows [21;p.87]:

> On the banks of the river at a league's distance from *Casas Grandes* we found a settlement ... where we counted

130 souls to whom we preached eternal salvation. The priest baptized nine children. They had fear of the soldiers and horses since they had not seen them until this time.

On the 19th [the next day], after mass, we continued to the west over arid plains. On all lands where these buildings are located there is no pasture. It seems that the land has a saline character. After having traveled four leagues, we arrived at a settlement called Tucsoni Moo, named thus on account of a great mound of wild sheep horns piled up, looking like a mountain. These animals are so plentiful that they are the people's common source of sustenance. This pile of horns is so high that it is higher than some of their houses. It appears as if there are more than 100,000 horns. The heathen Indians welcomed us profusely, sharing with the soldiers some of their supplies. We counted 200 courteous and peaceful people...

We recall from Paragraph 10 of the Friar's narrative that the people of Totonteac wore clothes of wool which they obtained from animals the size of Castilian greyhounds. Surely here is the source of that wool. The great number of those sheep suggests that they had been domesticated by the former inhabitants and preserved as a resource; presumably that mountain of horns was not the product of the tiny village which then occupied the place. On the basis of this great herd of sheep, then, let us tentatively identify the ancient province which surrounded the Casa Grande as Totonteac.

The central regions of Arizona continued wild and raw for a great many years after the passing of Father Kino in 1711. As a consequence of the Mexican War of the 1840's and the Gadsden Purchase of 1853 the region came under the jursdiction of the United States, and settlers began to arrive. However, because of hostile Apaches, the colonies did not prosper until the end of the Civil War when the Army moved in to enforce peace upon the region. In 1867 Jack Swilling noted the remains of ancient canals leaving the Salt River, and seeing the possibilities, he decided to undertake farming by irrigating lands remote from the river itself. He acquired a modest backing, and the Swilling Irrigating and Canal Company was formed to deliver the stuff of life again to the parched land. This first project reclaimed lands in the valley of the Salt River which were situated about 40 miles to the northwest from the Casa Grande; this structure, we recall, is near the Gila River.

Soon small farms dotted the newly irrigated area, and since barley and pumpkins were the chief crops at first the budding new town came to be called Pumpkinville. But eventually the 300 residents decided that their little community deserved a more dignified name so a town meeting was called for the purpose of selecting one. Darrel Duppa, an Englishman of considerable background and learning, is usually credited with the suggestion which was finally adopted. He recounted to the assembly the ancient legend of the Phoenix bird; it lived for five hundred years, was consumed by fire, and was then reborn anew from its own ashes. Duppa felt that Phoenix would be an appropriate name since, as was plainly evident to all, the new town was rising from the ashes of an ancient civilization. The residents liked his idea, so Phoenix it was.

The first methodical excavation of the ruins around and about the area was undertaken by Frank Hamilton Cushing in the years 1887 and 1888. The project was known as the Hemenway Southwestern Archaeological Expedition because it was financed by a Mrs. Mary Hemenway of Boston. Cushing set up his camp at a location about six miles south of the river and to the east of a range of rocky hills now known as the South Moutains. He called the site "Los Muertos"—that is, "The Dead". After three seasons of work at this one location the expedition shipped three railroad cars full of excellent material back to the Peabody Museum of Harvard, but more than 50 years passed before a report of the findings was published. By that time Cushing was long since dead so one must search elsewhere to learn of the opinions he formed from his own on-site observations. We shall return to consider them later.

While the Cushing party made careful note of the Los Muertos site and the ancient canals serving that region south of the Salt River, the remainder of the valley was not so carefully studied. The townsfolk at large were not greatly interested in matters of the forgotten past, or, if they were, their interest took second place to the immediate task of preparing the land for farming. Although some of the old canals were preserved and put to use almost as they were found, and others were used in part, most of them were filled in, and new ones were constructed. Consequently not much remained of the old system after a few years; and where the ancient cities intruded they also were put to the plough, usually with few records being kept. In 1929 one old-timer recalled how it had been in those former days [41;p.21]:

> ... At that time [1887] if a balloon could have passed over the valley, the ancient canals would have been as conspicuous as the highway roads. The only difference between the ancient and modern was the absence of running water. They could be traced and mapped as fast as the observer could pass over the ground. At that time in determining the sale price of land, the acreage of prehistoric canals thereon was customarily computed and deducted, since the cost per acre of grading-in the canal was as much and in most cases more than the selling price...

It is a great tragedy that this destruction continued for some considerable time before anyone thought to make a careful record of the ancient system as a whole. In fact, it was not until 1903 that James W. Benham [3] produced the first detailed map which attempted to trace the courses of all the canals in the old system. That map is reproduced on the

The Sequel

end papers of this book*. The scale can be reconstructed from the large squares (township boundaries) which are six miles on a side. It is important to keep in mind that the system was far from intact when this map was drawn— although Benham said that he based his work on observations which had extended over many years. Companion notes were written by H. R. Patrick [30], and the combination of map and notes was published as Bulletin No. 1 of the Phoenix Free Museum. Patrick himself had been a resident of the region for twenty-five years, and he also had studied those remains as best he could so we can hardly do better than to hear him at length.

> The size and capacity of the canals are quite surprising, the largest being seventy-five feet wide between the centers of the borders and probably not less than forty feet wide in the bottom of water under way, with borders about six feet in height being quite equal to any canal of the present system.
>
> The longest canal is about twelve miles in length but one of the old systems has about twenty-eight miles of mains, while in the agregate there are one hundred and thirty five miles of main in the old system. While the total mileage of the modern systems is but ten miles more.
>
> The acreage of land under these old systems is approximately one hundred and forty thousand acres, which, if divided into small holdings such as the present Indians cultivated under their natural conditions must have represented over twenty thousand farms, and with a corresponding number of persons to each family, the ancient canal system must have supported a population of from 120,000 to 130,000 people,—but to this may be added a large population in

---

* *Let it be noted that the map has been edited slightly in order to use the space at hand most effectively. To this end approximately five eighths of an inch has been cropped from both the left and right edges. The legend has been preserved intact by moving it to the right appropriately.*

the cities who may not have been farmers or tillers of the soil, so that the population of the entire valley might easily have been 200,000.

Coming to the subject of cities and towns, we find them covering an extent of country about twenty five miles in length, east and west, and fifteen miles in width north and south.

The more important of these cities are seven in number, and are designated by the letters A to G on the map, and are noted for having one large principal building, probably a communal house or temple, around which are clustered from one hundred to two hundred small buildings, besides these there are seven or eight small towns or villages that must have contained a numerous population, and there are other isolated ruins that are scattered along or near the ancient canals.

So there were seven principal cities of old supported by that vast irrigation system in the valley of the Salt River. They all derived their vital water from the same source so one can easily deduce that they must have been confederated under a single governor—otherwise they could not have lived together in peace during times when the river was low. Can there be any doubt, then, that these were the seven renowned cities of Cibola?

It is sad to report that out of all those seven cities only a single, small residue of one solitary structure remains in evidence today. This was the principal building of the city denoted by "D" on Benham's map. The relic was named "Pueblo Grande", and it is now preserved as an archaeological site and museum by the City of Phoenix. One corner of this old ruin is shown in Plate 3; it is here viewed from the south with the modern Grand Canal being visible in the foreground.

The Sequel

PLATE 3: *Looking north at the Pueblo Grande with the modern Grand Canal in the foreground.*

Phoenix is bounded on the south by a range of low, rocky hills called simply the South Mountains. In its wildest state it was a barren, uninviting tract neither grand in its aspect nor pleasing in its verdure. Nevertheless, in the early 1920's a group of Phoenix residents were able to appreciate its potential as a park site, and they set themselves to the task of developing the region into a recreation area. South Mountain Park remains today mostly a wilderness preserve comprising in excess of 15,000 acres, but paved roads have made it accessible to the public. Picnic accommodations have been provided, and a number of trails have been cleared for hiking and horseback riding.

In 1926 a curious memento was discovered on the eastern slope of the South Mountains—a rude inscription, dated 1539, with the name Fray Marcos de Niza clearly legible! The location was held secret for several years until the property could be annexed to the park and the inscription protected against vandalism by a closely spaced grating of heavy steel bars. A photograph of the inscription, taken through these bars with a wide-angle lens, is reproduced here as Plate 4. The damage visible at the right was inflicted before the barricade was erected, and in fact, it may have occurred even while the writing was being made since it appears in the very earliest photographs.

Plate 5 shows the site with its protective enclosure from a few yards to the east, and one can clearly see the very

PLATE 4: *The Fray Marcos de Niza inscription on the eastern slope of South Mountain.*

dark color of the rocks which cover this hill. Even so, only a very thin crust near the surface is dark; the interior is much lighter, which is why the writing is so clearly legible. It has not been artificially enhanced in any way.

As might be expected, most authorities have branded this inscription a counterfeit—and not a very clever one at that. For Coronado, as everyone knows, passed far to the east and missed this spot by probably 150 miles. And of course the presumption was that it doing so he had only retraced the route followed earlier by Fray Marcos. But not only had the supposed forger placed his work far away from

PLATE 5: *Showing the site of the Marcos de Niza inscription and the protective barricade of heavy steel bars.*

the "proper" course, he had seemingly made an even more foolish mistake in his choice of text. In order to understand this problem, however, and to put it in its proper place, we must digress briefly and review a short but tragic chapter out of the early history of New Mexico.

In the years following Coronado's expedition a Spanish settlement was established in that new territory; Santa Fé was its capital. But in the course of time resentment mounted amongst the Indian population and eventually an embittered native organized a revolt against the Spanish rule. A rope with a number of knots was circulated secretly around the various Indian villages and was duplicated at each one. One knot was to be untied each day, and when none remained the white men were to be destroyed. As this worked out the appointed day was August 13, 1680, but word of the plot reached the authorities a few days ahead of time.

When the insurgent learned of this breach he ordered the attack to begin at once, so hostilities actually started on August 9th. About 400 settlers were killed, along with the priests, and only those few who were warned in time managed to survive and to work their way to Santa Fé. The capital could not be held for lack of supplies, but there were enough Spaniards present to enforce an orderly retreat; they moved south, about to the present site of El Paso. This is how it happened that by the end of the year 1680 not one white man remained alive within all of northern or central New Mexico. A few young children were spared, however, and were reared by the Indians.

Twelve years passed before the Spaniards were able to launch an effective counterattack. As has already been mentioned, the Spanish government did not normally finance campaigns of this kind. Instead, a contract was let to some man of means to undertake the task. If no plunder was likely then his reward would be in lands, titles, or other honors, and this case was no exception. The expedition was under the command of Don Diego de Vargas who was appointed

The Sequel

Governor and Captain General; he provided the necessary supplies and resources from his own personal fortune, which was extensive.

Now Burke [7;p.143 et seq.] has reported a great many details of that expedition. The General started north up the valley of the Rio Grande with a small band of troops in August of 1692, but he found all the pueblos along the way deserted, the inhabitants having fled. His first contact with Indians in this northern excursion was at Santa Fé where he arrived on the 13th of September. De Vargas was a capable diplomat, and he resorted to the force of arms only

PLATE 6: *The de Vargas inscription at El Morro National Monument, New Mexico. National Park Service photograph.*

as a last resort. Accordingly he was able to retake Santa Fé at the conference table, so to speak, without a shot being fired.

According to Burke, de Vargas left Santa Fé on the 21st of September bound for Pecos to the east. That pueblo retaken, also by persuasion, he returned to Santa Fé and then headed west. Sometime during this western campaign, before the end of that year, he caused the writing shown in Plate 6 to be inscribed upon a massive rock a few miles east of Zuni (now El Morro National Monument). The text is heavily abbreviated, but as presently understood it is rendered into plain Spanish as follows [see, e. g., Reference 2]:

> *Aquí estubo el General Don Diego*
> *de Vargas, quien Conquistó*
> *a nuestra Santa Fé y a la Real*
> *Corona todo el nuebo*
> *Mexico a su costa*
> *año de 1692*

The discerning reader will recognize that, excepting only for the date itself, the last three lines are identical to the writing on the rock in South Mountain Park. In English this becomes:

> Here was General Don Diego
> de Vargas, who conquered
> for our Holy Faith and for the Royal
> Crown all the New
> Mexico at his own expense
> year of 1692

As his second blunder, then, the supposed forger had slavishly copied the last lines of the El Morro inscription, being unaware of their true meaning. For clearly, if these words have been correctly interpreted then they are utterly out of place upon a rock in South Mountain Park!

But one ought to grant any supposed counterfeiter more devotion to his art than this would imply so it behooves us to examine the above interpretation very carefully, and indeed, several serious flaws are quickly apparent. For one thing, note that the small e above the first A in the third line of the inscription has been entirely ignored in rendering the text into clear Spanish. For another, the letters which have been interpreted as *todo* in the Spanish (all, in English) form not one word in the original, but two, and the second word or abbreviation is capitalized. And finally, while it was true that de Vargas financed the expedition, it would have been out of character for a man of his position to have mentioned it on a monument of this kind. It was the custom in those times for the commander to bear the cost so it was already understood and would not have been worth recording in this fashion.

But the first error is certainly the most serious and the root of all the difficulty for if the clear text is not recovered properly then the meaning must inevitably be confused. The third line, then, must start with a word beginning in A and ending with e, and that word is most probably a preposition. Only one possibility comes to mind; it is the word *allende,* meaning beyond. In that case *Nuestra Santa Fé,* which was rendered "Our Holy Faith" above, should not be translated at all; it ought to be read simply as the name of the capital city, and if so then the added word *nuestra* deserves some comment.

It is well known that the commonly used place names of Spanish origin in the New World are sometimes mere abbreviations of a more complete form, and in this formal name the word *nuestra* was often used where appropriate. Thus, for example, La Paz is more properly *Nuestra Senora de la Paz* (Our Lady of Peace) while Los Angeles is *Pueblo de Nuestra Senora la Reina de los Angeles* (City of Our Lady, the Queen of the Angels). In view of this custom, *Nuestra Santa Fé* would seem entirely plausible as the formal name for the city, but as we shall learn presently, this does not happen to be the case. Therefore it is necessary to assume that the scribe took a liberty in rendering the name. Since *Nuestra Santa Fé* is so apt it's possible that it was in truth commonly used at the time. And then again it is also possible that since he was a newcomer to the region the writer may not even have known the correct formal name for the city; he may simply have jumped to an obvious, though incorrect, conclusion.

Now the word *real* in Spanish has two meanings. As an adjective, of course, it signifies royal; but it can be used as a noun as well, and in that case it denotes the encampment of an army*. Indeed, the formal name of the city is *Villa Real de Santa Fé de San Francisco,* and it harks back to a former Santa Fé after which it was named. When Ferdinand and Isabella were in process of driving the Moors from Spain, the last Moorish stronghold to be besieged was at Granada. Here the soldiers constructed an uncommonly elaborate camp-city outside the city walls. So elaborate was this encampment, in fact, that they thought it deserved a name; it was called Santa Fé. It is interesting to note that Columbus proposed his voyage of discovery to the King and Queen while they were in residence at that first *Villa Real de Santa Fé.*

With this understood, the first three lines become:

> Here was General Don Diego
> de Vargas, who conquered
> beyond Santa Fe and to the encampment

—the encampment, that is, of his own army. In that case these three lines are complete in themselves; the next line must begin a new thought altogether, and the very construction seems to bear this out because in the Spanish language

---

* *According to present usage,* real *is deemed to be of the masculine gender so it should take the article* el, *but we note that the feminine article,* la, *is used in the inscription. Therefore this interpretation assumes that the usage in those days was not universally fixed. Presumably there were local, or dialectical variations in the article used with this noun.*

an adjective nearly always follows the noun it modifies. Accordingly, if *real* had been meant as an adjective describing crown then we should have expected the scribe to write *la corona real*. But he did not, giving additional grounds for interpreting *real* as a noun even though the article does not conform to present standard usage.

With these minor discrepancies, then, this interpretation not only agrees with the writing on the rock, it is also historically accurate. That is, it does not ignore that superscript e above the first A in the third line, and, as has just been seen, de Vargas did go beyond Santa Fé to the east to retake Pecos before turning around and going west. On the other hand, the currently accepted reading is not historically accurate since he had not retaken "all the New Mexico" by the year 1692. The campaign was only three months old when that inscription was made; he had only just begun. Furthermore, the prevailing interpretation requires an unlikely construction in which an adjective precedes the noun it modifies and an insupportable reading of the two groups, *to* and *Đo,* as a single word.

The meaning of the next two lines is obscure, but if they constitute a new context altogether then we shall be able to reach a satisfactory resolution of our present problem even without understanding them. However, if the word *su* (which was read as "his own") does indeed refer back to de Vargas then these two lines would belong to the previous context and all five lines would then have to be interpreted together. But *su* could just as well be read as "her" or "its", and *costa* also has a double meaning—it being the common word for coast. But this word seems to be applied in a broader sense in Spanish than in English, for let us recall Father Kino's usage in a passage quoted earlier:

> ... These certainly must be the Seven Cities mentioned by
> the holy man, Fray Marcos de Niza, who in his long pilgrim-
> age came clear to the Bacapa rancheria of these coasts,

which is about sixty leagues southwest from this casa grande,
and about twenty leagues from the sea of California.

Since the Bacapa rancheria was so far inland from the
sea (more than 60 miles!) it would not be a coastal settlement
as we would use the term. Moreover, he used the word in
the plural so evidently it is not the exact equal of its English
counterpart. Thus the fifth line might be interpreted:

Mexico to her coast

Obviously the sense to be given this phrase depends critically
on the meaning of the previous line—which in turn hinges
on the interpretation of $D\!\!\!\!D$, at present unknown. But it is now
surely plausible that these two lines are indeed independent
of the first three so perhaps their import can be discerned
even if their meaning is obscure. For if we assume for the
moment that the South Mountain relic is genuine then it
must be considered very strange that these two inscriptions,
separated in time by over a century and a half, should both
contain two unusual lines, in the same order and identical
even to the form of the letters.

Perhaps the crucial first step toward resolving this little
puzzle is to note that the first three lines in the de Vargas
inscription contain hardly a word that is spelled out in full;
those lines are characterized by their artful abbreviations.
On the other hand the next two lines contain only one
abbreviation, if we understand $D\!\!\!\!D$ to be such. But notice
especially that this one is executed altogether differently than
the abbreviation of the name "Diego" in the first line. This
variation in technique, coupled with the pronounced change
in the manner of forming that one solitary abbreviation,
suggests that the writer may there have been quoting from
another text.

Now de Vargas probably did not inscribe the writing
upon the rock himself although he may have directed that
it be done. Someone else executed it, and the very precise
form of the letters suggests that the writer was highly literate

and practiced in his penmanship, a priest without question. In fact, Burke [7;p.146] states that three priests accompanied de Vargas northward and that all were Franciscans—peas out of the same pod as Fray Marcos!

A glimmer of light peeks through for we can be confident that in addition to the narrative that we have already read, which was an official Spanish document, Fray Marcos would have filed a report of the journey with his own order as well. But it need not have been merely a copy of the other; in fact, we recall that Father Kino mentioned a "book" which Fray Marcos had written. His official report would hardly be called a book so the account written for his own order was presumably much more detailed. Perhaps he would even have reported the very words which he inscribed upon that rock above Cibola. Later Franciscans would have access to that book. Granting this much, who would say that those three Franciscans bound for that same country (so they thought) would have failed to read that document?

Accordingly, we find that the most plausible explanation for the correspondence between the two monuments is not that a counterfeiter copied the de Vargas inscription, but that the de Vargas scribe deliberately quoted the previous inscription as Fray Marcos had reported it. Presumably the scribe intended this token as a quiet tribute to his maligned brother of the cloth.

Now there remains just one more detail to consider. Recall that Fray Marcos stated he erected crosses along the way at each of the principal villages as part of the rite of taking possession for the King. In particular, he mentioned that he erected a small wooden cross upon the hill above Cibola. But might he have constructed still others as well? Although it is not commonly known there were formerly four stone crosses laid out upon the summit of one of the hills west of the inscription in South Mountain Park. They were discovered in the early 1930's by Charles M. Holbert, the Park Custodian. Since memory of these crosses has all but vanished, it seems worth while to record the salient facts about them as they have been pieced together from the accounts of two witnesses*.

When the Marcos de Niza inscription came to light, Holbert became convinced that the ancient cities which had formerly occupied the valley of the Salt River were indeed the cities of Cíbola. However, going along with Father Kino, he thought that they were long dead when Fray Marcos spied them and that ancestors of the modern Indians had then already partially resettled the lands. His great interest in the matter prompted him to express these views in a small pamphlet which he distributed at the park [19].

Now there was, and still is, a settlement of Yaqui Indians just east of the South Mountain range—the village of Guadalupe. These Indians were refugees from Mexico and relative newcomers, but they had become intimately familiar with the local terrain. Holbert was acquainted with a few of them, and he asked about stone crosses which might possibly exist in that region. His Indian friends told him that, indeed, there were four such crosses, but they refused to say where they were located. As it turned out they looked upon these crosses as a kind of shrine, or sacred place, and they were in the habit of burying small sacrifices in the earth around them.

But Holbert eventually found them anyway. According to his son, Holbert searched long and diligently for those crosses. He even flew back and forth over the mountains

---

* The first is Harry Holbert, son of Charles Holbert. The younger Holbert was not a resident of Phoenix, however, and never saw the crosses for himself; he tells what he heard from his father. The second is Pete Ferguson who replaced Holbert as Park Custodian upon the latter's retirement in 1939. Ferguson had worked with Holbert for a number of years prior to his taking over this position.

in an airplane searching from the air, but to no avail. Then on one occasion, while climbing near the summit of one of the hills, he leaped headlong over a small ledge to avoid a rattlesnake, and he noticed the alignment of stones there in the brush beside him where he lay. Holbert stated that the stones were uniformly coated with "desert varnish" when he found them so he judged that they had lain undisturbed for a very long time. He dubbed the site "Four Cross Hill", and he listed it afterwards as one of the attractions in the park [19,31].

But it wasn't long until word got noised about that there was Indian treasure buried under the stone crosses in South Mountain Park. Those were the dark days of depression, and since the hill had been identified the crosses did not long survive. And more's the pity since according to Holbert the sacrifices consisted only of such things as small pieces of turquoise, a safety pin, or an occasional small coin. It was far from a treasure since the Indians were as poor as everyone else.

According to Ferguson the crosses were formed from loose rocks upon the ground at the summit of the hill. The arms tended to be uniform in length, as in the Spanish ensign, and were typically 8 or 10 feet long. Both Holbert and Ferguson repaired the crosses after treasure hunters had damaged them. Sometime during the War, while Ferguson was serving in the U.S. Navy, Holbert, on his own, organized a community picnic for the purpose of repairing those crosses once more. This time the stones were set in concrete which was carried up the hill by bucket brigade! When the Marcos de Niza inscription came to be branded a fraud the crosses sank back into oblivion where they remain today. Present-day maps* do not mention the site, and very few remain

---

* *Even maps prepared by the Park Service in the 1930's indicated the location of the crosses only very crudely, so the author is unable to report here on their present condition. He has searched for them both on foot and from the air but has found nothing.*

alive who remember them at all.

Did Fray Marcos and his small party lay those stones out upon the hill? No one can now say, but someday without a doubt the archives of the Franciscan Order will yield up that second narrative which Marcos must have written. When it is found, then we shall know, but probably not before.

Chapter 4:

DEAD MEN

LET US RECALL that the Indians living around and about the Casa Grande in Father Kino's time thought that the former inhabitants had moved southward, having been weakened by prolonged wars with the Apaches. Other villagers in the extended area offered different opinions, but the more forthright admitted that they simply didn't know who those people had been or what had become of them. They were referred to simply as "Hohokam", and that has come to be their accepted name today. The most widely popular interpretation would have this Pima word signify "Those who have gone", and thus bring to mind a migration, or an exodus of the former inhabitants. But this is not the proper meaning of the word at all as Haury [17;p.5] has taken pains to explain in detail. This author points out that *Hokam* is the Pima word for anything whatever that is "all used up"; repetition of the first syllable forms the plural. Thus, the term could be used to describe the houses or the cities perfectly well since, lying in ruins, they were all used up. But the name is not applied to the cities. It is given to the people who occupied them. According to Turney [41;p.21], *Hokam* is the Pima word for a dead man, and this is obviously a specific useage which is perfectly consistent with the general meaning, for a dead man is surely all used up. Hohokam, then, signifies "Dead men". Perhaps the name was applied first to the cities and only afterwards to the people who had occupied them. But if it was given to the population from the beginning then presumably when first found the ruins were strewn with skeletons of the former inhabitants!

The cities which formerly occupied the valley of the Salt River, then, have been identified as the Cities of Cibola, while the region surrounding the Casa Grande fits well with the wool-growing province of Totonteac "to the southeast of Cibola". But also to the southeast should be found Marata, according to Fray Marcos, and indeed it is. The great ruin known today as Snaketown fits perfectly. Marcos also stated that Acus and other cities even larger than the seven lay beyond Cibola, and that points to the Verde valley as the likely site. This valley is narrower than the others but very long, and ancient ruins have been found along nearly the whole length and in many of the side canyons as well. Montezuma's Castle, shown in Plate 7, is an outstanding example, but there are many others. Residues have also been found along the Agua Fria River to the west. A simple map of the region is given in Figure 3; the locations shown for the Seven Cities have been taken directly from Benham's map on the end papers. The territory occupied by those people was immense, so as vast as was the picture painted by Fray Marcos of the Cities of Cibola and their neighbors, that picture fits easily within the frame at hand—a remarkable fact, and one not to be set lightly aside. How could it have happened, then, that this seemingly obvious association wasn't eagerly acclaimed from the beginning by everyone concerned with the matter?

The problem was fundamentally one of dating those old remains. We know that archaeologists today have very sophisticated means for determining the ages of cultures and artifacts, but early investigators were obliged to depend upon more indirect lines of reasoning. Often they were very indirect indeed, and that left room for a certain subconscious

PLATE 7: *This cliff dwelling is all that remains of what was once a moderately large village. It was dubbed Montezuma's Castle by the early settlers, and the name stuck although it had no connection whatever with that Aztec ruler. Now a National Monument near Camp Verde, Arizona.*

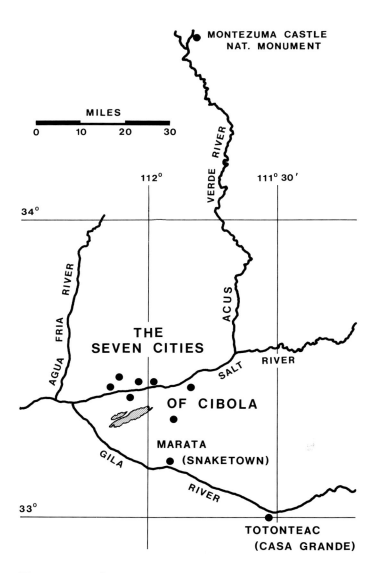

FIGURE 3

force to operate which may have colored their judgement somewhat. That is, we understand that the goal of an archaeologist is to search for and to study the roots of human culture. Presumably the very oldest remains would be of the greatest interest because they would throw the clearest possible light upon this important problem. And perhaps one can recognize a converse aspect to this yearning as well. In his enthusiasm, might there not be a corresponding tendency to estimate the greatest possible antiquity for the site at hand? Certainly no responsible investigator would ever knowingly falsify or misrepresent the evidence, but in the absence of definitive evidence, clues which seemed to indicate great age might in all honesty be given greater weight than others which pointed in the opposite direction.

One may be able to discern this force at work in the present instance by going back to the time of those first excavations and attending to the train of reasoning almost from Cushing's own lips, despite the fact that he was not privileged to speak through the official report published by the Peabody Museum. For it happened that a reporter from the San Francisco EXAMINER visited the site, and in a series of lengthy news stories he fairly well described the proceedings. Since these old issues of the newspaper are not readily available it may be well to quote here at length from one of the articles. The rationale by which Cushing arrived at an age for that Los Muertos culture is itself interesting, but other peripheral facts are mentioned along the way which are valuable as well. So let us now read exactly what the citizens of San Francisco read in their own newspapers on the morning of January 22nd, 1888. The article carries the headline "THE SEVEN CITIES" and after some preliminary remarks, the reporter tells us this [34]:

> ... When Cushing first began his work he was under the
> impression that he was dealing with but one city. In need
> of a name, he called it Los Muertos. But as the settlers,
> attracted by his investigations [and] the fertility of the valley,

began rapidly to clear their land, the discovery was made that with not one, but with many cities the investigator had to deal. By the time this fact was thoroughly ascertained, the essential character of the first city excavated, Los Muertos, was determined. It presented, indeed, a singular appearance. It consisted of an aggregation of large pueblos, or blocks, closely grouped together around a central temple or citadel building. Each pueblo was capable of accommodating from 1000 to 4000 souls, according to its size.

The term pueblo has been applied to that type of building in which those Indians who are the descendents of the ancient inhabitants of Los Muertos now reside. The ancient pueblo differs very little from the modern pueblo of the Zunis; indeed, the latter is as nearly as possible an imitation of the former. It consists of a huge building many stories in height and covering an extended area. Many of them are very much larger than one of our city blocks. The rooms are small, mere closets, so that with many stories the capacity of these pueblos is much greater than their external appearance would seem to indicate...

Here follows a discussion of the clan distinctions among the modern Zunis and strong similarities to the same which were found in these ancient ruins. Then he describes the oven and funeral pyre which is somewhat remote from the present topic, but after this he continues:

When Mr. Cushing was living at Zuni, Professor Adolph Bandelier, now the historian of the Hemenway expedition, was pursuing his ethnological studies in that quarter. Mr. Cushing, from his initiation into the Zuni tribe and priesthood, was recognized as an almost absolute authority in all matters concerning this interesting and primitive people.

Among other questions, Professor Bandelier asked him this one: "Why do the Zunis speak of the masters of the Six Great Houses. The Zuni town is one gigantic pueblo. What do they mean with their Six Great Houses?..."

..."All that I can tell you", said Mr. Cushing, "is that there are Six Masters of the Great Houses. One is Priest of the North, another is Priest of the South, another of the West, another of the East, a fifth is Priest of the Under-World; the sixth, the Priest of the Over-World or Skies. These six men, together with the Priestess, constitute the Supreme Council of the Zuni Tribe..."

The surprising fact, which it is the pleasure and the duty of the EXAMINER to communicate, is that the Great Houses of the Zuni Priests have been discovered... It is as strange and as interesting a fact as science affords that among the pueblos which constitute the cities of the Los Muertos system rise the six Great Houses of the ancient priesthood. Nay, there are seven houses corresponding to as many cities. The temple building, which is the central edifice of Los Muertos, Los Hornos, Los Pueblitos and the other cities, is the Great House of the ancient Priesthood. To the astonished members of the Hemenway expedition, this fact was at first regarded as startling coincidence, but a still stranger discovery increased the wonder. A hasty investigation of the great ruin near what is now Mesa City, revealed the further fact that in these ruins alone of the entire seven, there were not one, but seven temple buildings!...

The reporter goes on to elaborate on this system of sevens and its supposed mystical significance, then he comes to the question of the age of these ruins:

... How old are the curious skeletons, pictures of which have appeared from time to time in the EXAMINER? Curiously enough, we are actually able to form an approximate idea of their antiquity. Seven miles east of modern Zuni there is a curious group of seven cities which give us the strongest kind of proof of antiquity. A volcano eruption has filled the once fertile valley with lava. Against one of the cities the lava flow ran up on to the mesa and actually against the walls. The same flow, continuing down the valley, entered the mouth of the Zuni canyon. And just there is a curious fact. After the volcano had spent its energy and destructive force, after the molten rock had cooled, a living stream formed and rushed down the narrow opening of the Zuni canyon. The gentle action of the stream has, during the centuries of time, finally succeeded in cutting through the solid basalt at least four feet. None but geologists would realize how much is implied by this phenomenon. Taking the most conservative standard, that which Lyell applied to the Niagra Falls, not less than 6,000 years would be required to do this work. The pueblos, having been built before the lava flowed, must have been at least 6,000 years old and probably much older. But the type of their architecture is far more modern than that of Los Muertos, and these ruins occupy a position much further south in the course of migration. Therefore, we are furnished with many cycles of time with which to account for the rise of the cultures. Who shall say that civilized man in America is not ten thousand years old? The discoveries in the Salt River valley justify the statement. It is not easy to controvert the force of such geological evidence as is presented by the wearing down of the little stream in the Zuni canyon through the solid lava rock.

These passages have been quoted at length because they contain much firsthand testimony concerning the Hohokam ruins which is otherwise not available. Notice that the author concurs in the number of the cities. There were seven of them. We also learn that the ancient city which occupied the site of the present city of Mesa was the proud possessor of seven of those Great Houses and was therefore most probably the headquarters for the lord of the Seven Cities— that is, Ahacus, which Marcos described in Paragraph 13. This would be the easternmost of the seven as shown in Figure 3, or the one labeled "F" on Benham's map.

Let us recall that only one of those seven cities was actually named Cibola, and perhaps we can identify it from the fact that this was the first city encountered by travelers who crossed the desert coming from the south. Judging from Figure 3, one would probably expect them to have arrived first at one of the cities on the Gila River instead. But they did not, so apparently their course lay somewhat to the west, and their final approach to the Seven Cities was from the west as well. Presumably their route was fixed by the availability of water along the way, or it may simply have been that visitors were less welcome at Marata and Totonteac. Whatever the reason, the city named Cibola was most probably the one south of the (Salt) river, near the western end of the group—the one which Benham labeled "E". In that case, Fray Marcos could have looked down upon Cibola from the South Mountains (shown shaded in Figure 3) in agreement with his statement in Paragraph 23. This also locates Marata directly to the southeast of Cibola, in agreement with the information given in Paragraph 13.

Now Cushing, as we learned from the reporter above, was an initiate into the Zuni priesthood, and perhaps his opinion concerning the meaning of those sevens was correct. Since the artifacts that he uncovered had so many familiar features, there may indeed have been very close ancient ties to the Zunis; after all, there had to be some reason why there were six masters of the Six Great Houses! But having followed his train of thought we can easily see why he did not think to identify those cities with the Seven Cities of Cibola. For one thing, he had overestimated their age by perhaps 80 centuries!

Forty years passed, and Omar Turney, a former City Engineer, published a long and detailed study of the old canal system. Dr. Turney's lifelong specialty had been hydraulic engineering as applied to irrigation so his studies were especially welcome. In Part II of his excellent report he made frequent reference to another very interesting fact which greatly influenced early archaeologists in their attempts to date that early culture. He pointed out that the heads of those old canals now stood high and dry as much as eighteen feet above the water level in the river! The unavoidable conclusion was that the bed of the river had been eroded down by those eighteen feet in the space of time since the canals had been used. Here is an example [41;p.20]:

... In 1902 Canal Twelve remained just as it had been abandoned a thousand years or more, its head coming to the river bank and looking down eighteen feet to the sparkling surface below; a canal left high and dry on account of erosion. This canal is now paralleled by the modern St. John's which equals it in length.

A word or two of explanation may be in order before continuing with this line of the discussion. First of all, Turney had his own system of numbering those canals. His Canal No. 12 was the one Benham had earlier called Ancient Canal No. 1. Next, as already mentioned, the early settlers irrigated from the river and even made use of some of those same old canals. How did they do it if the river had eroded down so far? The method, simply, was that the new canals left the river at a very slight angle and ran nearly parallel for some distance, but at a smaller grade than the river itself. Because of that smaller grade the canal water gradually gained elevation over the level of water at the corresponding place in the river, and eventually it could be directed inland where, if desired, it could be made to flow in one of those ancient conduits. However the old canal thus served would originally have taken its head far downstream from the head of its modern feeder.

But the ancient inhabitants didn't have to resort to this artifice, for as Turney tells us explicitly [41;p.16]:

... All the canals start out nearly at right angles to the river, and run directly to the lands to be served; they give no evidence of having been run up the river bottom to a higher grade.

This great drop in the level of the river bottom speaks for an enormous span of time since the old canals could have been utilized. In order to test this conclusion Turney consulted with a number of eminent authorities in this study area whom he conducted to the river for an on-site inspection, and then he reported their impressions as follows—here let us keep in mind that the river bed was dry by that time since retaining dams had been built upstream; even so, the former water level could apparently still be discerned [41;p.36]:

> Standing in the boulder bed in the river, looking upward to the open channels of System Two above on the bluff, Dean Cummings, Professor of Anthropology of our State University, said, "It seems as though two thousand years were too brief an estimate of the time needed to create this change," and then thoughtfully added, "It is not enough." The Dean of our College of Mines and Engineering, Dr. Butler, a geologist, examined them and said, "The estimate [2000 years] is reasonable, very reasonable." The Professor of Astronomy, Dr. Douglass, the world authority on the record of tree rings, by using their testimony states that the abandonment might have occurred at the time of the later drop in rainfall between 500 A.D. and 600 A.D. or that it may have been before the beginning of the Christian Era. The Professor of Geography of Northwestern University, Dr. Haas, has said, "This river aggrades nearly all the year and degrades only during the short time of high water, the net degradation is small; probably more than two thousand years have [been] required for such channel erosion" ... That French trained specialist on paleolithic man, Dr. Renaud, of the University of Denver, standing in the eroded river bottom and looking at the mouths of System Two, summed up all the conflicting lines of evidence and stated his opinion that these canals could not have been used for fifteen hundred years. After all came Dr. Marvin, then President of the University of Arizona, and said, "All these estimates are far, far too recent, these canals came nearer being coeval with the power of the Pharaohs of Egypt."...

So this great erosion of the river bed is seemingly even more convincing evidence in favor of the great antiquity of that former culture. Perhaps one should not be surprised after all that those old cities were not quickly identified as the Cities of Cibola which Fray Marcos claimed to have seen alive and thriving in the year 1539.

THE LOST CITIES OF CIBOLA

As is well known, several objective and presumably absolute means for dating early cultures are available to archaeologists today. The radiocarbon method is probably the most widely noted, and it is often supplemented by a highly developed technique of correlating the growth rings in trees and timbers. However these modern methods have only added to the confusion surrounding the Hohokam because they show without a doubt that those people lived until a very much more recent time than had been formerly imagined. In fact, their demise is now dated somewhere in the vicinity of A.D. 1400! Now the magnitude of the problem becomes all the more evident for we have just heard a whole panel of experts deduce from the eroded condition of the river bottom that probably two thousand years have passed since those canals could have been utilized.

But an even more recent date is required for the fall of that nation if they actually were the same cities which Fray Marcos described. Accordingly, it must now be asked how firmly those objective methods determine the specific date A.D. 1400 which was given above. It turns out that the tree ring method of dating has been only marginally useful in the Salt and Gila River valleys since few trees and worked logs survived to be tested. It's probably a small loss since dates determined by that method must pertain most directly to the growth, or building stages of a community; they would correlate with its fall only by inference. Radiocarbon analyses, on the other hand, should be useful in dating all phases of the culture—even the very end of it. However archaeologists find the radiocarbon results to be strangely puzzling in regard to the Hohokam. Let us hear a long-time expert tell of his own experience with the technique. Professor Emil Haury is here speaking of a group of 32 radiocarbon assays made on artifacts taken from Snaketown (that is, Marata) during the years 1964 and 1965 [21;p.333]

> ... It would be an understatement to record that the results were in agreement with each other. The opposite is the

case. The task of sorting out those dates that appear usable from those which are obviously incorrect and justify one's selections is not simple. It is unthinkable, however, that dates for the Vahki Phase materials as far apart as 425±115 B.C. and A.D. 1020±120, or for the Sacaton Phase of A.D. 990±100 and 1820±110, can all be correct. These discrepancies force a choice. To do otherwise would land us in a chronological quagmire.

The reason or reasons for these disparities may be many, ranging from the selection, collection, and recording of samples in the field, to contamination, and analytical errors in laboratory processing, and even to the assumptions on which isotope dating is based. It is not my intent to try to determine where the problem lies. However, I firmly believe that in making a qualitative judgement about the value of dates, an intimate knowledge of field problems and of the nature of the cultural complex under study is fundamental to the decision... My dependence on certain radiocarbon dates and rejection of others will not be pleasing to everyone, but these judgements must be made. If the complications arising from the establishment of a chronology of Snaketown, involving only a few millenia, have taught us anything, it is that we are far from having reached a finite level of expertness in the art of dating as applied to archaeology.

Haury tabulated the results of the remaining 31 of those 32 radiocarbon measurements, omitting the Sacaton Phase sample which had indicated a date of A.D. 1820±110 years. Now Sacaton is the name given to the most recent phase in the culture at Snaketown, and fortunately his list contained three more samples from that phase. After making the small correction implied by the tree ring calibration he gave dates for these three of A.D. 935, 965, and A.D. 1660. Prof. Haury estimated that the last date given may be accurate to within a hundred years as is customary for good samples stemming from the 17th century.

Of course, one would not expect all the samples to give

exactly the same age because the various phases represent intervals of time, not specific dates. Also the radiocarbon assay itself is subject to error, but the wide variation in these dates does seem anomalous as Haury very plainly states. Somewhat later in this discussion we shall find at least one plausible accounting for the discrepancies, but for the present, despite their questionable accuracy, let us merely note that the Sacaton Phase results cited above do support a substantially more recent date for the fall of those cities than is presently acknowledged. In fact, in light of Haury's illuminating remarks above, it is easy to conclude that the date A.D. 1400, which is presently given for the end of that former culture, represents but an uneasy compromise between the objective evidence newly available and the older ideas of extreme antiquity.

Now one can understand how it happened that the Hohokam cities were never identified as the cities of Cibola despite the fact they they answered the description so well. The main reason, of course, is that the Friar's enthusiastic account had long since been set aside as a fanciful lie—and why not? Marcos himself publicly identified the Zuni pueblos as Cibola and, in effect, confessed to having greatly exaggerated many points in his earlier description. The cities of Cibola were therefore not even candidates for discovery.

But the second reason for not suspecting this relationship is that the age of the Hohokam cities was vastly overestimated from the very beginning, an error brought on mainly by the highly degraded condition of the ruins in even the earliest of modern times. They were mere mounds upon the desert floor, and in the arid desert, where erosion is slow, this implied great age indeed. Of course Cushing's estimate, based as it was on an assumed rate of erosion of an unrelated lava flow in New Mexico, was entirely unfounded, but other indications of great age had to be taken more seriously. For one, by actual observation it could be determined that up to 18 feet had eroded away from the river bed since the days when those cities could have been occupied, and that would have required several thousands of years, at least, if the erosion rate had been normal and constant all the while. Surely in such a context men can be forgiven for not thinking to identify the Hohokam cities as Cibola.

But still another troublesome factor has stood in the way of making this identification, for if it should be supposed that the Hohokam cities actually were alive and thriving as lately as 1539, then the riddle of their demise seems to be altogether intractable. That is, what could possibly have happened to them in the short span between 1539 and 1694, when they were first seen dead and leveled to the ground? In the absence of a plausible answer to this difficult question there is very little temptation to plead this otherwise obvious possibility because the problem of explaining those cities into oblivion is hard enough as it is. It should be noted that while current opinion places their ultimate end some-where in the vicinity of 1400 or 1450 A.D., one is not required to believe that they were actually flourishing at so late a date; in fact, the migration, or the decay, is thought to have begun long before so no strict time limit is imposed upon the processes of erosion by this point of view.

But in light of our present results, this identification of the Hohokam cities as the cities of Cibola and their neighbors is not a matter choice but one of stark necessity. When properly understood, every single item of pertinent evidence requires it. One cannot plead that more data is needed to resolve the point because the data in hand is already sufficient. The point is resolved! Gone, therefore, are those added centuries which gave erosion time to act at leisure upon abandoned cities and reduce them to ruin. Now a mere 155 years span the transition from a flourishing metropolis to a barely recognizable wasteland, so the awesome conclusion is unavoidable—the cities of Cibola and their neighbors were suddenly and completely destroyed by some enormous catastrophe, the nature of which cannot even be imagined at this time!

Consequently the problem of their demise is one of an entirely different magnitude than has been suspected. Nevertheless, despite the passage of years and the encroaching civilization, we shall be able to progress against it and perhaps ultimately, to some degree, resolve it. However the fact of those 18 feet missing from the river bed should give warning that its solution will be in corresponding measure surprising. And indeed, in order to comprehend it at all one is obliged to open his eyes somewhat wider than before and to adjust his vision well beyond its accustomed range. Thus girded to expect the unexpected, let us return to the scene and continue with the investigation.

Chapter 5:

A Flat Canal?

EARTHQUAKE comes readily to mind as one possible cause for the destruction of those cities and the fall of the river bed. Perhaps the land rose by 18 feet during the cataclysm; then the water would erode its bed to a new depth in making its way to the sea. As a matter of fact Cushing himself was of the opinion that earthquake had brought an end to the cities, but he thought that the inhabitants had only migrated to some other locality because of one. His theory was that those Indians had a deep longing to live at the perfect center of the world, and since the perfect center of the world would presumably be free of earthquakes then even a minor temblor would be looked upon as proof that they had not yet arrived at that ideal spot. They would move on in search of it. But where on earth could they have gone? We recall that Cushing was an initiate into the Zuni priesthood, and that may have been the reason why he looked for a sublime interpretation of the signs when a more ordinary one would have brought him closer to the truth. It is not necessary to agree with him on this point, but one should note his reason for thinking that an earthquake had occurred nevertheless. This also is to be found only in the newspaper, so let us rejoin that same reporter in that same edition of the San Francisco EXAMINER as he begins to explain that supposed migration:

> Mr Cushing's explanation for this phenomenon [that is, for the migration] has not perhaps been thoroughly understood. There is an impression gone abroad that the City of Los Muertos was destroyed by earthquake and the inhabitants killed. Such a theory is essentially ludicrous and sensational. There is no doubt that the walls of Los Muertos were severely shattered and often thrown down by great earthquake. There is no doubt that many of the inhabitants were killed by falling walls. An illustration of such an accident is given in the EXAMINER today. But, serious as was the disturbance and unfortunate as were the consequences of the earth's upheaval, there was a far more important reason which impelled the migration of the people, a reason which sprang from the very bowels of their philosophy and religion...

We need not pursue it. The point is that it was easy to see that the walls had been thrown down and that people had been crushed under them. A drawing made from a photograph of one of those victims accompanied the reporter's words. We had already deduced from those conflicting signs at the Casa Grande that the cities had been physically destroyed, and here are first-hand observations which confirm the fact. We had also deduced from the name Hohokam itself that the cities' residents had been killed on the spot; here again is corroboration. Surely one cannot imagine that the overturning of those walls occurred at any other time than the last days of that city. If the city had survived the episode then there can be no doubt that the rubble would have been cleared, the walls would have been repaired, and the victims would have been burned or buried according to the customary rites as a comfort to their families. But none of these things was done. The walls lay where they fell.

It is interesting to note that although Cushing himself discounted the idea that an ultimate catastrophe had overtaken the nation ("Such a theory is essentially ludicrous and sensational."), others who were present and who examined the evidence for themselves did not take such a restrained view. Why else would the reporter have written: "There is an impression gone abroad that the City of Los Muertos was destroyed by earthquake and the inhabitants killed."? Present-day archaeologists discount these signs altogether because Arizona is not subject to severe earthquakes. Gentle disturbances have been felt on rare occasions, but at least within modern times it is unlikely that serious damage to man or property has ever resulted from one.

Furthermore, if one considers the evidence available today then he must conclude that no such wide-scale shift has occurred, because a variance in the level of the land by those 18 feet would certainly have rendered the courses of those ancient canals invalid. Now it's true that the evidence was already far from complete by the time careful note was taken, so many of the routes shown on Benham's map had to be deduced from mere fragments of the old canals and a knowledge of the present topography. But some of the ancient conduits were put to use by the early settlers almost as they were found, and they worked perfectly well—proof enough that no general shifting of the terrain has taken place during the intervening years. The old courses, then, remain valid routes even today—in most cases, that is, and one of the apparent exceptions makes an interesting problem in its own right. Let us consider that one now.

Omar Turney, we recall, was a specialist in matters relating to irrigation, and he was greatly interested in that ancient civilization whose ruins were then so plainly evident on all sides. Consequently it was only natural that he should have thought to test those early farmers as hydraulic engineers. With this end in mind he systematically measured their canals for form and grade in order to learn how well they understood the principles involved. Most of their canals were very well designed indeed; modern engineers could do no better, but in one instance especially he encountered a remarkable puzzle—it seems that the old conduit had essentially no grade whatever, yet it ran for more than 12 miles! This was the northern-most canal of the old system in the western portion of the Salt River valley, the one that Benham had called Ancient Canal No. 5.

Turney compiled and published a map of his own which went through five editions, and upon that map he pointed out this strange feature explicitly. Plate 8 is an enlarged segment of his first edition map of 1922 [40], and Plate 9 shows the same region on his fifth edition version of 1929 [41]. Notice that for the most part he reproduced the course

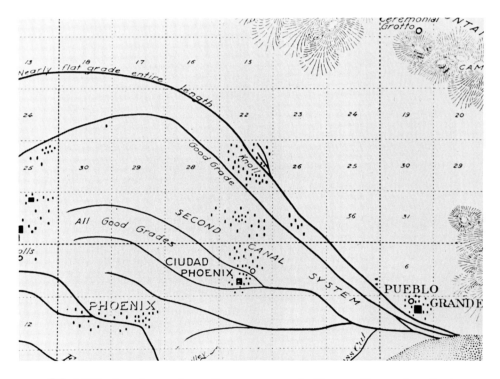

PLATE 8: *An enlarged segment of Omar Turney's first edition map (1922) of the prehistoric canal system in the valley of the Salt River.*

which Benham showed for this mystery canal, even to the branching features around that small knoll. The two versions of his map are almost the same, but they differ slightly with respect to some details near the Pueblo Grande. By eliminating one of the branches here he gained a canal head at the river, and in 1929 he called that site the "Park of Four Waters" in honor of this new addition.

One can hardly imagine that Turney intended any deception by making this change, so presumably we can safely "read between the lines" and conclude that the evidence was either incomplete or ambiguous in this region. The

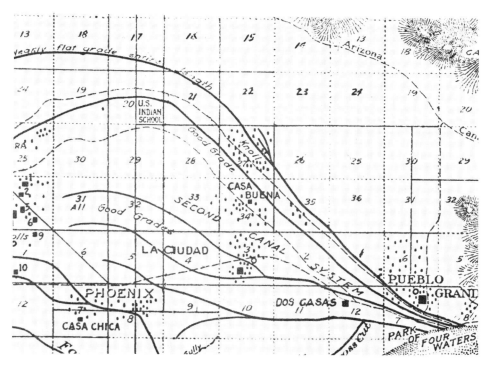

PLATE 9: *The same region as in Plate 8 as rendered on Turney's fifth edition map of 1929 showing notable changes near the Pueblo Grande.*

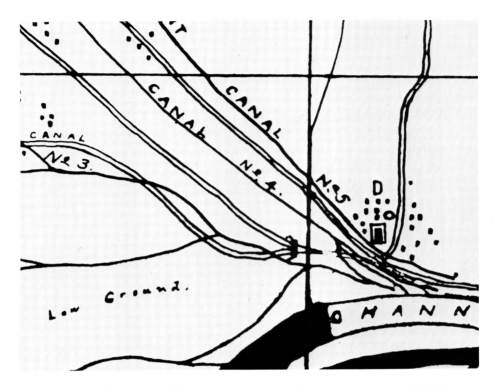

PLATE 10: *An enlarged segment of Benham's map of 1903 showing generally the same region as in Plates 8 and 9.*

original canals in that area being no longer in evidence, considerable deduction was necessary in order to reconstruct the courses as indicated. In 1922 he agreed with Benham for the most part, but he changed his mind later on. This should give warning that some portions of these maps are merely guesswork; they are not everywhere strictly reliable.

Plate 10 is an enlargement of the corresponding portion of Benham's map. Let us note in passing how these two authors showed the courses of the modern canals; Turney indicated these with dashed tracings while Benham used parallel solid lines. Although the names of the modern conduits do not appear in these small segments, one can easily recognize the modern Grand Canal as the one passing close to the Pueblo Grande (compare Plate 3).

Now as one studies Plate 10 he must note a very strange thing, namely, that Benham showed neither three nor four, but only *two* canal heads at the river in this vicinity! There appears to have been a minor question about Canal No. 3 so he left it incomplete, just short of joining with the others. But this Mystery Canal No. 5 comes to an abrupt end well away from the river with no prospect of a head whatever. This seems extremely odd for although the ancient system was far from complete in his day, Benham did not hesitate to fill in missing portions in other areas. Why should he have hesitated here? Apparently he was aware of some fundamental problem with the evidence—one that he struggled with but could not resolve. Let us try to reconstruct his thinking and attempt to deduce what that problem might have been.

Irrigation canals must be laid out in harmony with the local topography, so let us first examine the constraints at hand. The valley of the Salt River is a gently sloping bottom land most of the way downstream from its junction with the Verde to its end where the Salt empties into the Gila (Figure 3 shows the lay of these rivers). One notable interruption in this regular terrain is found in a narrow span of rolling, rocky ground on the eastern reaches of the city of Phoenix; Plate 11 is a view towards the south looking down upon this area. Notice that it is dotted here and there with a number of small buttes of an uncertain character. Since the land is useless for agriculture it has never felt the plough, and much of it remains in its native condition even today. A large portion has been set aside for recreational purposes, having been named Papago Park after a nearby tribe of Indians. This elevated region extends all the way to the river just a few hundred yards upstream from the Pueblo Grande.

Benham, then, had residues of that northern canal at hand, and he set out to reconstruct its course so that he could enter it on his map. His task should have been an easy one. Given the grade that a functional irrigation canal requires, he had merely to trace backwards along such a grade from the last clear residue until he arrived at the river.

But that higher rocky ground evidently presented an insuperable problem. In principle he might lay out a plausible route to a head sufficiently far up the river, but the virgin surface in that region testified loudly against it. That ground had not been disturbed, either by the modern settlers

PLATE 11: *A view toward the south looking down upon the span of rocky ground at the eastern boundary of Phoenix.*

or by the Indians before. To avoid that obvious conflict with the evidence, then, he picked out the route shown, but in doing so he arrived at the river too far to the west—that is, at much too low of an elevation.

Instead of laying out this canal at ground level, might the Indians have constructed a kind of elevated aquaduct and then continued on to the east to a higher head? Perhaps they followed substantially the same route as did the builders of the modern Grand Canal in this region. But evidently Benham satisfied himself on this point too, for barely twenty-five years had passed since work began on this modern conduit. Even if written records had not been available to him, many of the workmen who took part in building the Grand Canal were still alive. They could have told him for certain, from their own firsthand knowledge, if the new canal had been build upon the ruins of an old one. There can be no doubt that their testimony on this question was firmly in the negative, because Benham admitted defeat rather than entertain that idea.

In later years Turney analyzed the problem somewhat differently. He was willing to assume a head for the canal in the vicinity of the Pueblo Grande and simply acknowledge that the conduit did not have adequate grade. He thought that the Indians were so desperately in need of more land for agriculture that they were willing to pay the very high price for water that this fault implied. But would this option even have been available to those farmers of old? It is not likely, because there can be no flat irrigation canal. These vessels are required to transport water, not merely contain it, and they need an appreciable slope in order to be useful at all—all the more so here since these canals had no lining. Water continually seeped through the bottom along the way, so a substantial rate of flow would be required near the head merely to supply this leak in a canal that was twelve miles long!

In plain words, then, the two maps agree on this remarkable testimony: In the early days, when the signs were fresh, a segment of an ancient canal remained in evidence which was entirely cut off from the river. That is, there is no feasible route, consistent with the present contour of the land, along which that downstream segment could have received its water. The problem is so clearly defined that its solution is all but forced; we can now be only one step away from understanding, but before taking that last step there is one additional item that must be considered.

Although nothing whatever remains of that mysterious canal today, some tangible evidence relating to the problem has survived. As it happens, of all the many miles of ancient canals which once coursed over the Salt River valley only three short segments still exist, and one of these is at the so called Park of Four Waters. The relics can be seen in Plate 12, this being a portion of an aerial photograph made by the U. S. Geological Survey in 1967 [42]. Let us note some of the main points. The curve along the very bottom is the northern edge of the river bed. Those black segments on the right, at the edge of the river, were sewerage treatment ponds; the ancient canal residues are the undulating features which border the river to the left of those ponds. Notice especially the pronounced "spur" which extends out to the right from this undulating region. Further to the north, near the center, one can make out the railroad line going east and west, while the Grand Canal passes under the tracks and works its way to the northwest. The old crosscut canal curves into it just above center, and one can just make out the Pueblo Grande residue there at the junction just above the very small bridge across the canal. Finally, then, Washington Street passes across the top of the picture.

The old residues have suffered much during the intervening centuries, both from man and from the elements, so they are difficult to interpret even on the spot. Plate 13 explains them nicely. This sketch was drawn by Frank Midvale, a long-time student of the old canal system, shortly

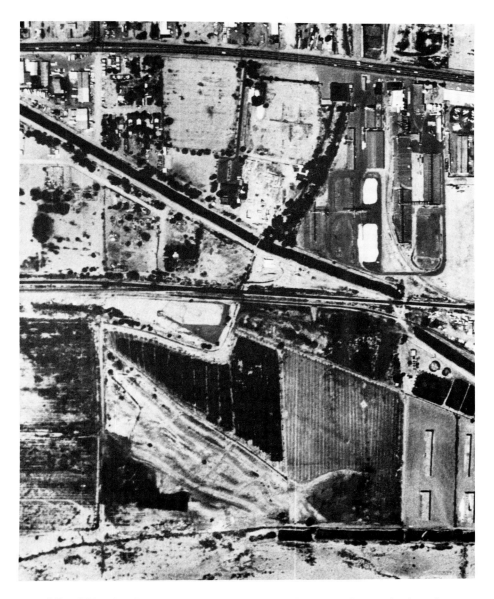

PLATE 12: *Segment of an aerial photograph made by the U.S. Geological Survey in 1967 showing the "Park of Four Waters" region.*

before his death. Midvale's personal papers and notebooks are now in custody of the Department of Anthropology at the Arizona State University in Tempe, and this drawing was photographed from amongst those papers. Notice that Midvale did not indicate the spur-like extension visible in Plate 12. This also has fallen victim to the times. It was subsequently destroyed to make way for an overflow sluice from the canal to the river bed.

At least today there are only two canal heads in that vicinity, and it is easy to conclude that most probably there were never any more. Presumably these two canals were

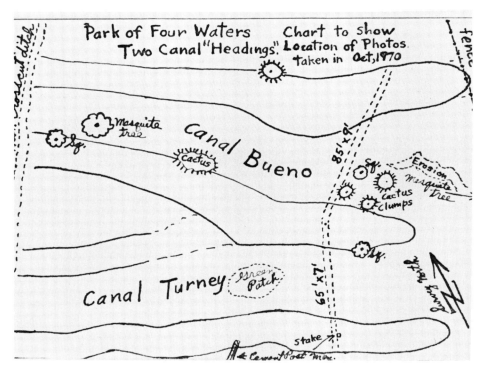

PLATE 13: *Sketch by the late Frank Midvale of the ancient canal residues at the "Park of Four Waters".*

joined at their heads so they could be fed together during seasons when the water was low. At such times the Indians would have been obliged to construct diversion dams across the river to raise the water level, and both of these heads could have been fed from behind the same dam. That spur-like appendage testifies that these were the actual heads of the canals. It would have diverted water into the canals, and it would help prevent flooding in the region to the north. One can now appreciate Benham's meticulous attention to detail all the more for it appears that he even indicated this spur on his map. As a point of interest, Plate 14 is a view

PLATE 14: *Looking into the head of one of the ancient canals at the "Park of Four Waters".*

from the river bank looking into "Canal Turney", as Midvale called it. The levees have been considerably degraded, filling in the channel somewhat, but when new it compared favorably with its modern counterparts. Note the dimensions that Midvale gives in his sketch. It was an enormous construction project for people who had only stones for tools.

So the two heads which Benham indicated still remain, adjacent as one would expect, and why should there have been any others nearby? Another canal would have been useful only if its head were far enough upstream to accept water at a significantly higher elevation, and in that case it would have required its own diversion dam or it could not be fed when water was low in the river. Such dams probably would have been built of rock and brush so they would wash away with the spring flood and would have to be rebuilt anew each summer. Consequently, they would have been thoughtfully spaced along the river so that each one would be worth the effort that went into making it. Since the river is a mile wide in this region, one would not expect another dam site near at hand; he would probably look for the next one considerably further upstream, several miles upstream perhaps.

So it becomes ever more certain that the course shown on these maps for the upstream portion of Ancient Canal No. 5 cannot be correct. Indeed, the indicated course can only be understood as the veiled statement of an unresolved problem. It is also certain that no solution to this problem is remotely feasible within the context of the present lay of the land. Yielding to the evidence, then, only one alternative remains: Ancient Canal No. 5 must have had its head well upstream from the Pueblo Grande, and it passed normally through the Papago Park region. *The high ground could not then have existed!*

Chapter 6:

MARKS OF A TRAGEDY

W E STAND POISED at the edge of that elevated region which is Papago Park and environs. Surely the next move is to examine it for corroborative signs—signs which might betray the nature of the tragedy that befell Cibola. But before entering to investigate let us pause for a moment to fix our present position firmly in mind. As a matter of fact the train of reasoning to this point consists of only six short steps, most of which are so easy that they would hardly be worth mentioning if their cumulative implications were not so profound.

First, then, faced with two conflicting statements by Fray Marcos de Niza concerning the Cities of Cibola, the one duly sworn and attested and the other by hearsay through Francisco Vázquez de Coronado, we chose to credit the first and to discount the second. To explain the discrepancy is to justify the choice, but even in the absence of justification the sworn statement should take precedence over the mere rumor. The next three steps are interpretations of ambiguous passages in the Fray Marcos narrative. To begin with,

2nd, that noteworthy point by the sea where the coastline turns sharply to the west was identified with that character-istic feature at the 28th parallel. Undoubtedly there are many sites along the coast where the trend is briefly westward, but only two stand out, and of these only the one satisfies the necessary conditions.

3rd, we assumed that Paragraph 13 of the Report was composed at a site two days' travel removed from that notable point by the sea, placing the jumping-off point for Cibola about 80 miles to the north. The village at that site was therefore identified as the precursor of Hermosillo.

4th, it was assumed that the "15 long days' travel" to Cibola was scheduled according *the Indians'* customary rate of progress, which was taken to be 20 miles per day instead of the 15.5 miles per day normal for the Spaniards.

With these four interpretations the Cities of Cibola are identified without ambiguity as the former Hohokam cities which were situated in the valley of the Salt River in central Arizona. No possible objection can be raised because these satisfy every detail of the description, and no other plausible candidate cities are anywhere in evidence. In that case,

5th, since the cities were flourishing in the year 1539 and lay dead and desolate barely a century and a half later, they must have been destroyed outright sometime during the interim by a large-scale calamity as yet unknown. But then we perceived a clue to the nature of that calamity, for

6th, it appeared that an important element of the ancient irrigation system had been reconstructed in error. The residues had been misconstrued because an upstream segment of one of the major canals had been entirely covered over by new dirt and rock, thus giving rise to the high ground now partially occupied by Papago Park. Of course, the origin of this new dirt remains to be determined.

It is gratifying to note that this line of reasoning also gives a plausible accounting for those 18 feet missing from the bed of the river. That is, since the elevated region of Papago Park extends south to the river and even beyond, the river would have been blocked by the fallen material at this point, and a lake would have formed upstream. But eventually, as the water level rose, this dam would give way and a rushing torrent of water charged with rock and gravel would have torn at the river bed and flushed it away. Damage would have been more pronounced downstream from the site at first, but in the course of time the erosion would retreat upstream to leave the river bed in the condition we find it today.

Let us enter that elevated region now and examine the terrain closely. Figure 4 is a simplified map of the area showing the features which have been discussed so far. As already noted, the river is now dry most of the time since retaining dams have been built upstream. Water is metered out as needed into trunk canals which follow along the northern and southern edges of the valley; the Arizona Canal, shown in the Figure, serves the area north of the river. The water is delivered to the Grand Canal via a cross-cut canal passing down the eastern flank of Papago Park and then through a tube under the high ground. This is how we happen to see water in the Grand Canal today even though there is none in the river. Benham's map shows where this canal originally had its head. It had to begin far upstream in order to supply water to approximately the same land the Indians once irrigated with canals starting out just below the Pueblo Grande. As already mentioned this strategem was necessitated by the intervening loss of those 18 feet from the river bed.

Referring again to Figure 4, the dotted curve outlines the region where the terrain is most notably rocky and uneven. There is no distinct boundary, but the land does become more regular in the area beyond, and the elevation gradually decreases until it joins smoothly with the normal contour of the valley. On the west there is nothing to show where the deposition of new dirt might have ended; but on the eastern flank the slope from the elevated region opposes the general trend of the valley, and the two grades meet at an arroyo which floods after heavy rains. This has lately been named Indian Bend Wash, and it is so indicated on

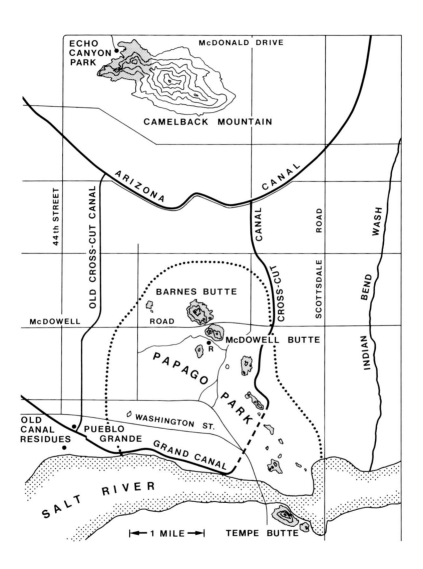

FIGURE 4

the map. Before venturing into the Park itself, it will be worth our while to pause and examine this eastern slope region briefly. The surviving evidence is meager indeed, but nevertheless signs are not lacking which suggest that the ancient topography was locally very much different than we find it today.

Plate 15 is the portion of Turney's map of 1929 which describes this area. Note that the author indicates residues of a small ancient settlement slightly west of that gully— where sections 2, 3 and 11 come together. If that little settlement had been built upon the presently existing surface of

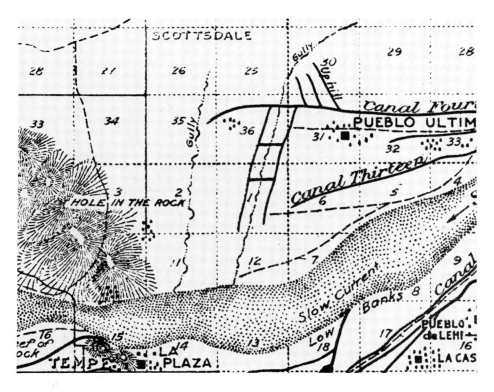

PLATE 15: *A segment of Omar Turney's map of 1929 showing the region to the east of Papago Park.*

the land then, of course, it would be decisive evidence against the reconstruction offered here. But it need not have been on the surface. The very gentle slope of the land here indicates that the deposition petered out and became very thin near its limits so structures in this area could still have been evident under this slight covering. Notice that Benham showed the wash to be quite wide on his map, as indeed it is, because the slopes on both sides are very gradual*.

In this context let us recall H. R. Patrick's observation (on Page 62) that the ancient Indians preferred to locate their villages next to the canals—a very natural choice to be sure, because they would need water for themselves as well as for their crops. But notice that if the present topography had prevailed in those days then that little village would have been without water altogether. Nor could crops have been irrigated in that region since no canal could have crossed the gully. Why, then, should the village have been there at all? On the other hand its water requirements could have been met very well indeed if the Mystery Canal, or one of its branches, had passed this village after leaving the river. We find no indication of a canal head in that vicinity on the maps, but such a residue would probably have been so heavily degraded shortly after the assumed fall of dirt as to be rendered unrecognizable. Presumably it would have been overtaken by the lake which formed behind the blockage in the river, and wind-driven waves would have eroded the banks until there remained only two parallel paths of rock and gravel running along a gentle mound of sand. Portions which lay within the Indian Bend Wash would, of course, have been carried away completely.

---

* Perhaps it should be mentioned that this region is now completely urbanized so there is no hope whatever of examining it anew with this picture in mind. Even Indian Bend Wash has partaken of the change. Because of the occasional flooding it is unsuitable for permanent structures so it has been laid out in picnic grounds, tennis courts, a golf course and other recreational facilities.

Marks of a Tragedy

It also seems significant that one of those ancient canals (Canal Fourteen, as Turney numbered them), after having followed a westerly course from the river, came to an abrupt end at this gully. If the wash had existed in those olden times then obviously the canal could have gone no further, but it is certainly not clear why the Indians should have constructed a main canal leading up to a ravine. In fact, this residue gives a fairly broad hint that the arable land continued further to the west in those days. And one can hardly fail to notice still another awkward feature upstream on this same canal; namely, three branches leave toward the north running uphill! The map points this out explicitly for only one, but presumably all three suffered from the same defect. Because of this fault, Turney was much more restrained in his praise of those old engineers when discussing these remarkable relics. In fact, he put it this way [41;p.18]:

> Clearly they were unable to determine where water would flow except by digging a channel and from such inability they could know little about the land to be reclaimed until completing the work. Let cease the boasting about ancient engineering skill; in few points only was it developed; a maximum velocity with the least earth removed was obtained by making the wetted perimeter bear a minimum ratio to the cross-sectional area. Long practice may produce results equal to technical skill.

Since we see those olden days only dimly it is all too easy to imagine that the Ancients were less than bright and themselves saw the light of day only dimly. But if they were able to discover that the wetted perimeter should bear a minimum ratio to the cross-sectional area in order to achieve the best flow for the least dirt removed then should they not also have discovered how to lay the course for a canal by digging small test ditches in advance of the main construction? They would have learned that very well indeed because they were a thriving community of practical farmers who successfully irrigated many tens of thousands of acres.

Perhaps one can account for this strange inconsistency by noting that if a canal were buried by dirt sifting down from above all traces would be lost when the covering became sufficiently thick. But on the edge of that fall, where the added material was not so thick, the bottom of the canal, its banks, and the surrounding terrain would all be covered to about the same depth. So the contour of the canal would still be evident at the surface; only its grade would be modified. In fact, with respect to the new surface the visible channel would run uphill for a distance before it gradually disappeared—and that is exactly what we see here! In this case, presumably, one would visualize a minor, localized fall of dirt which was somewhat isolated from the principal event. Although no accounting has yet been offered for the source of that dirt, nevertheless a plausible understanding for this puzzling bit of data is to be had within the same context as for the central problem.

Returning now to the map on the end paper, note that Benham also indicated an ancient habitation just north of the river in the Park region which Turney, in Plate 15, later showed as a fair sized village. Now this site is decidedly on high ground so if there actually had been an ancient settlement here then the present hypothesis certainly would be untenable. But to this writer's knowledge only one of those sites can be identified today, and we see it in Plate 16. The photograph shows little except for the size; the structure was quite small, possibly the work of one man. The ground is high and very rocky so this was not the abode of a farmer, and the isolation does not square with the Indians' customary manner of living for they were a communal nation. Although the walls have fallen a few of the foundation stones are still in place, and they betray a crude, light construction which further suggests the work of an individual—one bent on satisfying only his own limited needs; it has not the substantial character of the Indians' work which aimed for permanence. The residue suggests, therefore, that the house

PLATE 16: *Residues of a small dwelling on the high ground of Papago Park just north of the Salt River.*

was that of a white man in a frontier environment; presumably it was the hermitage of an early settler.

The terrain in the immediate vicinity of this relic is raw and uneven and remains today essentially in its native condition. Consequently, if other habitations had ever existed here then their traces should also still be in evidence, but nothing else is to be found. Benham's suggestion of a settlement at the site (and Turney's enlargement upon it) was therefore based on exeedingly thin evidence which seems to have been misinterpreted. This being the case, it is natural to wonder if the small village considered earlier, the one shown on the western slope of Indian Bend Wash, could have been similarly misconstrued. It may indeed have been a shallowly buried village as assumed here, but on the other hand it, too, might have been erroneously inferred from residues actually stemming from more recent times. Unfortunately we shall never know for certain since all traces in that area were destroyed long before careful records were kept.

Now it is evident that demonstrable residues of the ancient culture anywhere upon this high ground would disprove the present thesis, but it is equally clear that the apparent absence of the same speaks strongly in favor of it. We saw earlier that if the present topography had prevailed in ancient times then there would have been no reason whatever for a settlement on the western slope if Indian Bend Wash. The same can be said for the Park region north of the river where the terrain is high and remote from arable land. It is therefore not particularly significant that these areas are devoid of genuine signs. But on the contrary, we certainly should have expected the Pueblo Grande and its surrounding city to have been situated—not on prime farming land near the river, but instead, given such an easy option, on the otherwise useless ground a half mile to the east where it would have been secure against flooding as well—had that high ground then existed. (Note the proximity of this high rocky ground in Figure 4 and in Plates 8 and 9.) Significantly, however, this high ground shows no sign of ancient habitation whatever.

Let us return to the central topic now and direct our attention to the elevated ground within the park region itself. Here we find a rolling, undulating topography which is interrupted here and there by the strange buttes seen earlier in Plate 11. These little hills differ markedly amongst themselves both in form and size, but despite their differences there are features which tend to be common to them all. Plate 17 shows a well-known example. The fluid contours are widely typical, but the deep caves prevail only toward

PLATE 17: *The butte commonly known as "Hole in the Rock", a picnic site attraction in Papago Park.*

the northern end of the park. This particular butte is known as "Hole in the Rock" because the large cave near the top extends all the way through to the other side.

The rock making up these hills would be classed as a "breccia", meaning that the mass is not a single large rock but many small ones that fit neatly together to form the whole. The size range of the component grains varies from one hill to another. In McDowell Butte the largest are granite blocks that must weigh several hundreds of pounds, while in some of the others they are mere pebbles. In all cases, however, the size grades down to a very fine silt which passes easily through a 300-mesh screen. Strangely enough, all of these elementary granules are individually coated with a thin layer of red pigment which is presumably some oxide of iron. This ever-present pigment accounts for the dark, somber aspect of the buttes which is so plainly evident. When this pigment is removed, for example in acid, the resulting particles are found to be mainly light, quartzose grains, angular as if freshly crushed, and to all appearances commonplace.

Plate 18 brings us closer to the main region of interest with a view looking toward the northwest at the large hill

PLATE 18: *A view of McDowell Butte looking toward the northwest. Barnes Butte is visible at the left.*

Marks of a Tragedy

just south of McDowell Road. Not previously named, this one has been dubbed McDowell Butte in Figure 4 because we shall need to refer to it often in the future. A portion of Barnes Butte is visible in the background, and Plate 19 is a full view looking north at Barnes Butte alone. Upon noting the layered structure of this hill, one's mind tends to spring far back into the distant past and imagine detrital material collecting in vast seas which later drained away. The soft contours suggest prolonged weathering and erosion while the level of the land gradually changed, tilting the bedding planes upward. The shallow, cave-like holes which

PLATE 19: *Barnes Butte looking north. From this aspect it displays clear bedding features tilted up to the right.*

PLATE 20: *A small canyon near the western end of McDowell Butte, looking north.*

dominate the surface suggest a wind sculpturing process— erosion by the driven sand, again continuing through untold ages of time.

Such might be given, in all fairness, as a "standard" interpretation of these features, but it could hardly be more seriously in error. If we observe the details closely we must find that the rounded aspect of these hills had an altogether different origin; in fact, we shall discover no evidence of erosion whatever. As will be apparent, these hills remain today exactly as they were the day they were formed!

Plate 20 is a view looking north into the small cleft

in McDowell Butte from about the position of the picnic ramada indicated by the dot at the letter R in Figure 4. Again one sees the cave-marked, rounded surface, but notice especially the dome-like projection just to the right of center. There can be no doubt that it is rounded because on some past occasion a portion of the rock became liquified and flowed downward! Plate 21 shows this same dome from a somewhat closer vantage point. One can easily discern that a viscous mass oozed over the top of the cave at the upper right and congealed as it was about to fall. The bridge across the left hand end of this cave must have had its origin in

PLATE 21: *A closer view of the dome-like structure visible in Plate 20 showing superficial flow patterns in the rock.*

PLATE 22: *A feature in McDowell Butte just to the right of the region of Plate 20 showing clear flow patterns.*

a similar flow from above. Evidently some of the liquid continued downward, and the resulting rivulets congealed shortly afterwards, even while they were running down the wall. Careful inspection removes all doubt. These actually are the patterns of a flowing liquid!

Clear evidence of fluid behavior can also be observed on the prominence in Plate 22; this structure is situated just to the right of the region displayed in Plate 20. One's eye is immediately captured by the globule affixed to the wall near the center. The fluid evidently flowed downward along the slanting ledge from the left. Apparently this course

PLATE 23: *A closer look at the caves on the left side of the small canyon shown in Plate 20.*

became blocked when the material began to congeal near the end, and the flow became progressively diverted over the edge. In fact, the entire face of that prominence, to the right of this globule, is thinly coated with congealed fluid which spilled over from the top. This added layer stands out because it is of a notably darker hue than the original rock, which is still exposed to view near the bottom.

Plate 23 is a view of the left side of the small canyon seen earlier in Plate 20. Several places are evident where gaps have been spanned by relatively thin structures which must have been liquid at one time. These forms are especially interesting because they indicate more than a mere flowing, or melting of the existing material; they appear to be the congealed residues of an added thin fluid layer which draped over the hill. The covering formed a kind of curtain over one cave near the center of the the picture, but it evidently lacked the strength to support itself so it broke apart over the larger holes leaving residues which can still be seen clinging to the tops of the caves.

Plate 24 is a view of that curtained cave from the other side of the cleft, or small valley. The presence of new material added over the old is very clearly revealed in this

PLATE 24: *The "curtained cave" visible in Plates 20 and 23 viewed from the other side of the small canyon.*

view. Also worth mentioning here is the fact that although the surface at large displays clear evidence of fluid behavior the individual components show no sign whatever of having been melted. The sharp angularity of the larger rocks at the surface is plain even at a glance in this photograph, but this property is not limited to the larger rocks. All sizes, even the smallest grains, are likewise sharp and angular. Clearly, then, this was not a melting of the familiar kind, but a phenomenon of a different order altogether. In due course we shall be able to discern a plausible basis for it, but for the present let us be content merely to explore some of its consequences.

Perhaps one can point to this strange melting effect as the origin of the great strength of this mass of rock. It has already been mentioned that, generally speaking, the grains are not cemented or fused together, yet they fit so intimately that they form an exceedingly hard, impervious whole. Nevertheless, once the surface is broken the mass can be reduced to its elemental grains with hardly more than finger pressure alone. Presumably the fit is so perfect because the individual grains at one time flowed to fill the available space compactly, but they failed to actually fuse together because of the ever-present coating of red pigment.

Let it also be noted that the sharp angularity of these superficial rocks speaks volumes for the youth of the structure at large, for no erosion whatever can be discerned in them. Even the delicate flow patterns, composed not of solid rock but of a frangible breccia, have survived almost in their pristine condition. And more significant still, the red coloration of the hills themselves persists even though it derives not from a color inherent in the rock, but from a mere coating of the individual grains. This point will be examined again later in another context.

Still other sites are readily accessible which display interesting flow patterns and also speak clearly for the youth of this new material, so let us work our way around the hill and examine some of them. Plate 25 shows McDowell Butte as it appears from the west looking east; the prominence observed in Plate 22 is visible here at the extreme right. The left side commands our attention now, and Plate 26 gives a closer view. Here the camera is stationed on the southern slope of Barnes Butte and is pointing in a southeasterly direction. Notice that rock decidedly in a fluid state has eased over the top of the right hand end of the cave on the lower right, and here, too, the fluid appears to have been part of a new layer which continued up the hill to form a partial curtain over one of the upper caves. Presumably

PLATE 25: *A view of McDowell Butte looking directly east. The region shown in Plate 22 is visible at the extreme right.*

it was a continuation of the same sheet that we observed on the other side of the hill. Further to the left the fluid appears to have been formed less like a sheet and more like two heavy "cords" which are plainly visible from afar, as in Plate 25. One can discern these cords as bulges above the lower cave, and there is an obvious dribbling of the liquid down the back wall as well. Plate 27 gives a closer view of this dribble.

PLATE 26: *The northwestern region of McDowell Butte as seen from the slope of Barnes Butte.*

PLATE 27: *A well-defined dribble of melt-rock running down the back of the cave near the lower center of Plate 26.*

Certainly one can discard out of hand the thought that this feature might be an accretion structure which resulted from the long-continued precipitation of minerals out of water trickling down the hill. Note that the cords are elevated above the general contour of the surface so they are not feasible water courses. Water might collect and flow between them, but not upon them. Furthermore, the texture is not that of a mineral deposition; indeed it is not unlike that prevailing generally over the surface of the hill. Neither can one suppose that this nicely defined feature could have been sculpted by the degrading processes of erosion. This is a small structure in itself, yet even its finest details remain perfectly preserved, giving added assurance, if more were needed, that these hills remain today in substantially their original form. Nothing of significance has eroded away.

It is interesting to note the continuation of that same sheet of overlying melt-rock upon Barnes Butte just to the north. Plate 28 shows this hill from the east looking west. The stark contrast between these pronounced fluid contours and the tilted, layered structure which this hill displays to view from the south (Plate 19) is noteworthy in itself. Plate 29 gives a closer look at the region on the left. Note how

PLATE 28: *Barnes Butte looking west. Note the contrast with the southern aspect shown in Plate 19.*

PLATE 29: *A closer view of a region visible in Plate 28 showing familiar flow patterns in the rock.*

new material has bridged the gaps in some places, but elsewhere the sheet has broken apart to form the now-familiar dribble features.

The texture of this newly added surface sheet tends to differ markedly from that of the underlying material—as this latter is revealed, for example, in the walls of the caves. In particular, the surface layer seems to be of a finer, tighter, firmer texture than is found underneath, and the coloration contrasts sharply as well. Indeed, the walls of the caves seem to have been as if thickly painted with a kind of pigment, perhaps similar to that which gives color to the surface, but of a somewhat paler hue. The presence of this coating tends to obscure the finer details of both composition and structure so that little can be seen of either. Plate 30 is an attempt to illustrate this unexpected coating. The photograph shows a small area near the back of one of the lower caves appearing in Plate 26; a postage stamp has been affixed to the wall to give an impression of scale. Notice the sharp contrast between the newly exposed face of the granite and its uniformly "painted" surroundings.

Being near the back of the cave, this site happens to be well protected from the weather, but instances can be found

PLATE 30: *The internal wall of a cave showing contrast between the paint-like coating and recently exposed granite.*

where this type of coating is at least moderately well exposed, and yet is still intact. One is therefore tempted to conclude that it is inherently characteristic of the caves and never did prevail at large over the entire surface of the hill. Its origin constitutes a little mystery in its own right—one, however, which does not need to be addressed at present. In a later context we shall deduce a plausible accounting for these caves, and that insight may cast some light on this riddle as well.

Now the dirt within the park is also very interesting in this regard since it, too, is of a reddish hue—and for the same reason as before; the individual particles are universally coated with that same red pigment. The color is less conspicuous upon the surface where the ground has not been disturbed, so some weathering is apparent, but even here it is unmistakable. Only in the arroyos where occasional running water and mutual abrasion have accelerated the weathering process are clear, unpigmented grains to be found. Since nothing of substance has eroded away from the buttes the pigmented ground material cannot have been derived from them; nevertheless it most probably came from the same unknown source as did the colored particles of the buttes. Presumably, then, the ground and the hills are of the same age. It is also interesting to note that the dirt here is a distinctive mixture of silt and gravel in which the sand-sized particles and the very small clay-sized particles are both notably scarce. This gives the particle-size distribution a characteristic bi-modal form which the writer has observed widely throughout the park area.

There remains now only to examine the region at the river where that proposed blockage would have occurred. Plate 31 is a view looking toward the south at the northern slope of Tempe Butte from high ground north of the river. The form of this small mountain is quite different from that of the buttes in the park itself, so one has cause to wonder if it is actually part of the same system. But whether

PLATE 31: *The north slope of Tempe Butte as viewed from high ground north of the Salt River.*

or not the mountain is of the same age as the park, ground material characteristic of the park region extends across the river and onto its slopes. That same mixture of silt and gravel, the individual grains being coated with that same red pigment, can be found well up on the mountain. Figure 5 is a particle-size analysis of a sample of dirt from this site. It is given as an example rather than as a comparison, of course, but it agrees with other analyses made in the park as well as they agree amongst themselves. Since the texture is so remarkable, the sand-sized particles being so notably scarce and the grains being colored as before, one

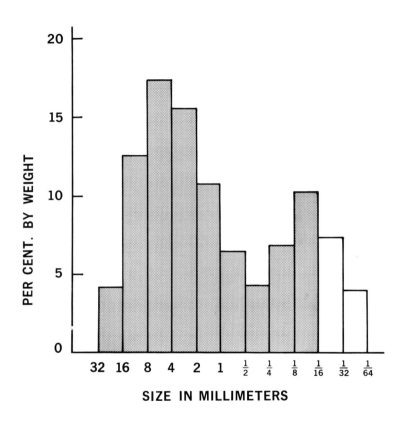

GRAIN SIZE DISTRIBUTION–SOIL SAMPLE

FROM NORTH SLOPE OF TEMPE BUTTE

FIGURE 5

has reason to be confident that this same material* fell continuously across the river, perhaps to block it as assumed.

Recall that we ventured into Papago Park looking for signs of the unusual only because our hypothesis was itself unusual. Presumably so bizarre a phenomenon as envisaged would have left traces behind which could not be readily understood in ordinary terms. Perhaps we had no right to expect anything but the most ambiguous of clues—subtle hints which might have been laboriously argued into some measure of corroboration for the picture. But what has been found is far from subtle; no labor at all is required to demonstrate the bizarre on all sides. Certainly the commonly recognized earth-shaping processes played no part whatever in producing these remarkable features; they can only be the product of some wholly unfamiliar phenomenon, the nature of which cannot even be guessed from past experience. Furthermore, the excellent state of preservation of even the finest details shows that the event must have taken place fairly recently. One would not otherwise know exactly how recently, but since it answers the call so appropriately it is very easy to conclude that this was indeed the event which destroyed the Seven Cities and their neighbors around.

---

* *The finer components, below 2 mm, were separated with the standard soil analysis sieves manufactured by Humbolt Mfg. Co. of Norridge, Ill. Below ½ mm the screens are not graded in fractions of a millimeter, although they closely approximate the sizes given in the figure. They are graded by mesh number—that is, wires per inch, the finest ones being numbered 60, 140 and 300. The figure shows two additional grades beyond these which are unshaded and which together comprise 11.4% of the total mass. This is the portion which passed through the 300-mesh screen, and the allotment of this 11.4% into the next two grades is assumed. Clearly, the bi-modal character of the distribution is very well defined however this allotment may be made.*

Our quest for Cibola has ended, but we were too late. Only her ghost was there to greet us, while upon the ruins stood those curious buttes in the Park like monuments to the dead. Thus does one mystery give way to another even more perplexing: What great tragedy overtook those many cities? What awesome holocaust could have destroyed them all so completely?

Without a doubt those enigmatical flow patterns in the rocks constitute the essential clue to the riddle, so our hope now is to learn to "read this writing on the monuments" that we might eventually come to understand what happened here. At this point it might seem a forlorn hope, because the signs are so utterly foreign to all previous experience. But surprisingly enough, gratifying progress can be made because somewhat similar signs are to be found elsewhere in another context altogether—fortunately, in a slightly more revealing context. The next two chapters will be devoted to a study of this other "context", for in the light thus gained the markings in Papago Park will not seem so hopelessly foreign after all. But before setting out on this side excursion, let us finish with our survey of the sites of interest here at hand.

At least as far as can be observed locally, rocks of the type in question are unique to Papago Park, with only two exceptions. One of these, known as Twin Buttes, stands alone about two and a half miles southwest of Tempe Butte, but since it seems to offer nothing particularly new it need not be considered further here. However the other locale does warrant careful attention. This is the "head" region of Camelback Mountain, a prominent landmark at the north-eastern limit of the city of Phoenix; the similarity of rock forms here to those occurring in Papago Park has been indicated by the shading of this area in Figure 4. Plate 32 is a telephoto view of this hill taken from the top of Tempe Butte. The smaller hills in the Park can be seen in the foreground, but owing to the narrow angle of view only the

Marks of a Tragedy

PLATE 32: *Camelback Mountain, with a portion of Papago Park in the foreground, as seen from atop Tempe Butte.*

eastern extremity of McDowell Butte can be seen, and Barnes Butte is out of the picture altogether. Even from this distance it is evident that the head region on the left is of an entirely different character from the rest of the mountain. Let us examine a few of its points of interest.

As Figure 4 indicates, even if only crudely, the head region encloses a small canyon whose southern wall forms a steep cliff. This wall is so contoured that it returns a clear echo so the site is called Echo Canyon, and part of it has been set aside as a park by the City of Phoenix. Plate 33 is a view of the small hill at the entrance to Echo Canyon

Park from a convenient vantage point on the south side of the canyon. The now-familiar fluid contours are plainly evident, and likewise the color and structure of the rock are similar to what has been seen previously in Papago Park, but it displays important new features which deserve our careful attention.

Let us examine the region at the end of the low wall surrounding the parking area; it is seen from the side in

PLATE 33: *The small hill at the entrance to Echo Canyon Park showing reddish coloration and familiar fluid contours.*

Marks of a Tragedy

Plate 34. Here the pre-existing surface has been coated with a frosting-like layer in which structures resembling icicles are distinctly visible, as at the lower left. Their remarkable inclination is of particular interest; instead of hanging downward as might be expected, they extend out almost horizontally as if they had been formed in a strong wind. Plate 35 is a closer view of the uvula-like structure hanging from the top of this shallow cave. The sharp angularity of the smaller rocks making up these forms is clearly revealed in this photograph. Thus, even as previously observed in

PLATE 34: *A structure near the parking area of Echo Canyon Park showing pronounced icicle-like features.*

PLATE 35: *Closer view of a feature visible in Plate 34 showing the sharply defined surface texture.*

Papago Park, despite the suggestion of fluidity on a larger scale, evidence of fusion is absolutely lacking on a small scale. One might therefore be tempted to conclude that these structures developed by accretion during a kind of condensation process.

And yet this view of the phenomenon will not suffice everywhere as the remarkable vista in Plate 36 very plainly demonstrates. Here the alien material lies in extensive pools on the northern "neck" region of Camelback Mountain. This new rock might be described as a bright red sand-and-gravel-stone, so it is of a substantially different kind than

Marks of a Tragedy

PLATE 36: *Alien reddish rock with prominent flow patterns on the northern "neck" region of Camelback Mountain.*

has been met previously. Plate 37 is a telephoto view of the region to the right of the steep cleft near the center. The impression of genuine fluid behavior seems to be well justified here because rivulets of this new rock are easily seen running over the side. The stark contrast between the fluid contours of this new rock and the jagged aspect of the native rocks in this area is plainly evident. Localized occurrances of this alien red rock are also to be found at the base of the neck region on the southern side of the mountain. And here forms suggestive of genuine melting, that is, of fluidity even on a small scale, are easily distin-

PLATE 37: *Telephoto view of an area visible in Plate 36 showing rivulets running over the edge of the cleft.*

guished—although they are not so easy to photograph because of the established housing.

Plate 38 shows a portion of the southern exposure of the "head" region of Camelback Mountain which manifests a flow pattern so gross that it can be easily overlooked. Note that the entire side of the hill has partaken of the fluid motion; the white house near the bottom seems about to be engulfed by the molten mass spilling over from above. One's attention is drawn especially to the cascade-like structure mid-way up the slope. As bizarre as were the forms seen thus far, this remarkable feature may be the strangest of

Marks of a Tragedy

PLATE 38: *A segment of the southern aspect of the Camel's head with cascade features frozen in the rock.*

all, because it suggests rapid movement with a high degree of fluidity—and yet the mass seems to have stopped instantly as if it had been frozen by the camera's shutter. The cascades did not even have a chance to flatten out!

With great difficulty one might bring himself to imagine that some very hot "torch" had heated this rock to melting, but it is completely impossible to conceive that such a great mass of molten rock could have cooled as quickly as these forms would indicate. In due course other examples of this unlikely behavior will be noted in Papago Park, and eventually we can expect to acquire a rudimentary understanding of it. But the time is not yet. More experience will be needed in this eerie quarter of nature or we might not even have the courage to understand. Let us pause, then, for a brief supplementary study—in a different context entirely—in order to gain that experience and the courage which should come with it.

Chapter 7:

YELLOW EARTH

THERE ARE TIMES when one feels the need for a guard railing lest he lose his footing and fall. In a figurative sense, this excursion may have come to the point where such a rail would be welcome because we have now reached a height never tested before. Is the path secure? Can one really believe what his eyes have just shown him? In the present circumstances a suitable precedent might serve as that guard railing since it would be something to lean upon along this unfamiliar way. The clues at hand are so perplexing as to make one despair of ever truly coming to understand them, but one should expect at least some progress toward this goal as his experience with the phenomenon continues to increase. With this expectation in mind, then, let us examine a candidate "guard railing" and see what can be learned from it.

Now even as the hills in Papago Park present a fairly ordinary face to an unsuspecting world, so also our hoped-for precedent seems so mundane as to be hardly worth a second glance—and yet upon closer scrutiny it becomes a mystery to rival anything that we have yet seen. Indeed, it is as strange a case as can be found anywhere in all the annals of geology. It is called the "loess", this being an anglicised form of its German name, *Löss,* the root of which is the same as for our word "loose"—which describes it aptly. Let us begin this study by quickly noting a few of the uncontested, universally recognized features of this interesting material.

For millions of people, upon four continents, loess is the very dirt beneath their feet. Nevertheless it is a very special kind of dirt. Its most obvious distinguishing features are its silty texture and yellowish color, but it has many other special features besides. As one can easily learn from an encyclopedia, it is localized into several broad areas around the globe. In the United States the deposit begins in central Nebraska and extends south and east to cover much of Kansas, Iowa and Missouri. It thins further to the north and east, but it extends to the south along the Mississippi valley and shows up especially well near Vicksburg and Natchez. Extensive deposits are found also in South America, notably in Argentina and Uraguay. Likewise, it is found locally in northern Europe and more broadly in central Asia, but by far the greatest deposits of all are found in China where the loess covers nearly a million square miles! In fact, to the Chinese yellow is the color of mother earth. The Yellow River derives its name from its burden of eroded loess, and the Yellow Sea is similarly colored by this same substance.

The encyclopedia also tells us that there is a small proportion of calcium carbonate (that is, calcite, the predominant mineral of limestone) present in the undisturbed loess which acts as a cement and binds the individual grains together. This gives the material a firmness that silt alone could never have. So firm is it in fact that in China very acceptable living quarters have been carved out of the loess deposits. But it is less firm when moist. Although calcite is not readily soluable it does dissolve slightly, so water frees the grains to some extent. Running water, then, removes the calcite entirely and quickly washes the silt away. As a consequence, streams of water easily erode through the loess

PLATE 39: *Exposed loess along Route 275 at Council Bluffs, Iowa showing well-defined vertical cleavage.*

and form their beds upon the firmer substrate underneath.

It is also an uncontested fact that the loess buries the pre-existing landscape like a blanket, hill and valley alike. Its thickness varies upwards from a hundred feet and down to the point where it can no longer be distinguished, and wherever found it presents the appearance of a massive, uniform deposit. Plate 39 shows an exposure of the loess along Route 275 in Council Bluffs, Iowa. One can also make out another typical and extremely significant property of the material in this view; that is, it has a tendency to cleave along vertical planes to form a bluff. This is quite general, and in fact the city of Council Bluffs derives its name from the loess bluffs which extend for miles here along the valley of the Missouri River. Plate 40 is a photograph made in China many years ago which also shows this surprising feature very clearly. The bluffs retain their form for many years, and when undermined by further erosion a section will collapse to yield a vertical bluff formation just as it was before.

This surprising tendency to cleave along vertical planes is due to the fact that the undisturbed loess, wherever found, is perforated with countless capillary tubules which are oriented mainly in a vertical direction. And here we come upon the first solid indication that this material is far from

PLATE 40: *An old photograph of loess bluffs in China. Reproduced from Plate XXIV of Reference 43.*

ordinary. How did this myriad of strange little tubes ever come to be formed? In fact, they are so unexpected that perhaps we ought to hear an eyewitness tell about them. The following description by Baron Ferdinand von Richthofen* was translated from the original German by the authors of Reference 43, and it reads as follows [43;p.183]:

> On every bit of loess, even the smallest, one may recognize a certain texture, which consists in that the earth is traversed by long-drawn-out tubes, which are in part extraordinarily fine and in part somewhat coarser; which branch downward after the manner of fine rootlets and generally are coated with a thin white crust of carbonate of lime. If one examines the loess in place one sees that most of these little channels are nearly vertical, yet branch at an acute angle and downwards, whereby an incomplete parallel structure is maintained. If one is looking at a loose piece, but not exactly at the surface of parallel fracture, one sees the ends of the little tubes which occasion an appearance of minute holes. But, apart from these definitely bounded elongated spaces, the earth between them has a loose porous structure and does not possess that close texture which is peculiar to other kinds of earth; for example, the clays, potter's clays, and loams.

Notice that the tubes actually constitute a key identifying texture of the material since they are to be found "On every bit of loess, even the smallest,...". Notice also that the baron described these tubes as "branching downwards after the manner of fine rootlets". Because of this branching, the most commonly cited explanation would have the tubes to be holes left by the roots of small plants which grew upon the silt while the formation was developing. Those

---

* *Modern geological studies of the loess actually began with Baron von Richthofen who published a treatise on his research in China in 1877. This now rare work was the ultimate source of the passage quoted here. Its author was an uncle of Manfred von Richthofen—the "Red Baron", famed German flying ace during the first World War.*

who support this idea point to the fact that tubes can sometimes be found with a root residue still inside. Without a doubt the presence of a dried root within a tube is persuasive evidence that that particular hole was formed by a root, but it would seem to argue just as strongly that the empty tubes must have had some other origin. A more plausible accounting for the uniform presence of these tubules throughout the entire body of the loess appears to be required, and one will be suggested in its proper place.

In his description above Baron Richthofen also mentioned another very significant property of this material; namely, he pointed out that the native loess is extremely porous, even apart from the tubes. In fact, according to Flint [14, p.252] the porosity generally exceeds 50 per cent—that is, more than half of its bulk is entirely vacant! One contributing reason for this strangely porous texture may be found in the unusually uniform size of the particles which make up the material. Most of the grains are in the size range of a fine silt, with the smaller clay-sized particles being rare and sand grains being almost nonexistent. Tight packing, of course, requires a broad range of particle sizes in order that the voids between the larger grains can be filled by smaller and ever smaller particles to form a compact whole. Because the component particles are so nearly the same size, that kind of packing is impossible in the loess, but even this cannot be the full reason for its great porosity. For when the binding cement is washed away and the silt is disturbed or redistributed the grains do settle together somewhat, the packing becomes more dense, and the material then resembles loess only in its color. In this condition it is usually called loess-loam, and it forms the basis of an extremely fertile soil—as farmers in Iowa are quick to boast.

The uniform size of the grains making up the loess, and the resulting inability of the particles to pack tightly together, makes the silt extremely vulnerable to erosion by the wind whenever it is once disturbed. When the binding

PLATE 41: *A scene from China showing deep erosion of a roadway into the loess. From Plate XXIX of Ref. 43.*

cement is lost, its strength also vanishes. Plate 41 illustrates one interesting type of consequence of this vulnerability to erosion that was once seen fairly typically in China. Here the road has worn deeply into the loess as the newly disturbed fine silt, leached of its binding cement, has continually blown away.

Scattered throughout the loess there normally occur peculiar nodules such as are shown in Plates 42 and 43. The Chinese call them "loess ginger" and the Germans, "loess dolls". They are especially rich in calcium carbonate, some being as white as chalk while others, containing less

PLATE 42: *Specimens of the characteristic limey nodules found scattered throughout the loess.*

calcite, are much the same color as the loess itself—as is the specimen in Plate 43. The peculiar surface texture of this one suggests that the nodules have an interesting story to tell also, but let us set them aside for the present and continue with this first introduction to the topic.

Although his original treatise is rare today, Baron von Richthofen reviewed his observations a few years later in a more accessible journal so we can hear this scholar describe, from his own firsthand experience, some of the properties that have just been discussed. His English is patterned somewhat after his native German so one must be especially

PLATE 43: *Another example of loess nodule, this one darker in color, with striking surface features.*

attentive in order to follow his meaning, but let us hear his own words* nevertheless [32;p.295]:

> Any theory which undertakes to deal with the problem of the origin of the Loess must give a valid explanation of the following characteristic peculiarities of it, viz.:
>
> 1st. The petrographical, stratigraphical, and faunistic difference of the Loess from all accumulations of inorganic matter which have been deposited previously and subsequently to its formation, and are preserved to this day.
>
> 2nd. The nearly perfect homogeneousness of composition and structure, which the Loess preserves throughout all the regions in which it is found on the continents of Europe and Asia; it offers in this respect a remarkable contrast to all sediments proved to be deposited from water within the last geological epochs, excepting those of the deep sea, which are here out of the question.
>
> 3rd. The independence of the distribution of the Loess from the amount of altitude above sea-level. In China it ranges from a few feet to about 8000 feet above the sea, and farther west it rises probably to much greater altitudes. In Europe it is known at all elevations up to about 5000 feet, at which it occurs in the Carpathians.
>
> 4th. The peculiar shape of every large body of Loess, as it is recognized where erosion has cut gorges through it down to the underlying ground without obliterating the original features of the deposit. These are different according

---

* Here, as on previous occasions and on several more to follow, evidence is presented in its rawest form—namely, as extended direct quotations from authorities giving their firsthand knowledge of the subject. Since their remarks are not always strictly to the point at hand, this is an inefficient means for passing along information, and it can be trying, too, because the writing is not always easy to follow. But passing along information is only part of the goal. The remainder is to offer the reader basis for sufficient confidence in his newly acquired information that he will feel encouraged to reason critically with it. For we shall find it necessary to be critical of the prevailing theory of loess deposition in order to improve upon it.

to the hilly or level character of the subjacent ground. In hilly regions the Loess, if little developed, fills up depressions between every pair of lower ridges, and in each of them presents a concave surface; but where it attains greater thickness, it spreads over the lower hills, and conceals the inequalities of the ground. Its concave surface extends then over the entire area separating two higher ranges, in such a manner as to make the line of profile resemble the curve that would be produced by a rope stretched loosely between the two ranges...

5th. The composition of pure Loess, which is the same from whatever region specimens may be taken, extremely fine particles of hydrated silicate of alumina being the largely prevailing ingredient, while there is always present an admixture of small grains of quartz and fine laminae of mica. It contains, besides, carbonate of lime, the segregation of which gives origin to the well-known concretions common to all deposits of Loess, and is always impregnated with alkaline salts. A yellow colouring matter caused by a ferruginous substance is never wanting.

6th. The almost exclusive occurrence of angular grains of quartz in the pure kinds of Loess.

Here is eyewitness testimony to one of the key features mentioned earlier—the loess spreads like a blanket over the former landscape, irrespective of elevation. He points this out directly as his 3rd property and then he amplifies upon it in the 4th. In fact, his words here might be used to describe a heavy snowfall just as well. The baron concluded his observations as follows:

There is but one great class of agencies which can be called in aid for explaining the covering of hundreds of thousands of square miles, in little interrupted continuity, and almost irrespective of altitude, with a perfectly homogeneous soil. It is those which are founded in the energy of the motions of the atmospheric ocean which bathes alike plains and hill-tops...

His language may be bit flowery, but the central idea is

plain enough; the silt must have filtered down through the atmosphere from above. It could not have been deposited by, or through water in any form—neither in seas, lakes, nor rivers.

Thus was born the so-called "aeolian theory" of loess deposition. At this point one should begin to feel the thrill of discovery, for surely that "covering of hundreds of thousands of square miles, in little interrupted continuity, and almost irrespective of altitude, with a perfectly homogeneous soil" cannot be set aside lightly as a triviality. Moreover, the fact that this identical material, complete with tubes and nodules, can be found on four widely separated continents presents a puzzle which confounds the imagination. Although the loess bears no outward similarity to the hills in Papago Park, perhaps one can be buoyed by the simple faith that two such remarkable phenomena—so bizarre but yet wholly different— would be unthinkable. They must have something in common!

The properties of the loess introduced above are beyond dispute; any adequate discussion of the topic must recount them all. Differences of opinion begin only with attempts to interpret these basic facts and deduce how the material came to be in its present form. Baron Richthofen suggested that the silt making up the loess in China had its origin in the Gobi Desert to the north. He thought the silt was a product of desert erosion which the wind had carried southward; presumably it sprinkled down upon the land as the wind lost its force. This idea has been refined somewhat in later years to fit it better to the individual locations where loess is found. For example, there is no vast desert in Europe to be offered as a source for the silt, but there are the residues of the continental glaciations so these have been proposed as the source instead. One common theory pictures vast flood plains formed by outwash from those melting glaciers. Then, when the water abated, and when the mixture of mud, silt and sand had dried, the wind is thought to have picked up the finer particles and blown them away.

Yellow Earth

The fine silts were presumably redeposited close at hand to form the loess accumulation, while the finest particles were distributed over a broader area and were effectively lost.

But this picture is beset with very serious problems. For one thing, it does not account for the calcite present in the loess which binds the particles together. If the supposed residue on that flood plain had contained grains of calcite (which the flood waters did not dissolve away), then, as the muddy mixture dried out, the particles should have been strongly cemented into a rigid mass which the wind could not have disturbed. On the other hand, if that residue did not contain calcite then where did the loess obtain its supply? Although the actual source of the silt assumed by this theory is altogether different from that pictured by Richthofen for the loess in China, nevertheless one should note that the wind still plays the key role. Supposedly it picked up the silt from one place and dropped it down in another in order to give rise to that blanket-like covering of the former landscape.

In the United States we have both the western deserts and the glaciation residues in the north, and each has its defenders as the source for the silt. But it might be well to recall again the essential conditions which Richthofen insisted must be satisfied by any plausible theory of the loess. For one thing, he required that any valid theory should account for the fact that the properties are the same regardless of the locality where found. It is not possible to understand how this same end product (complete with tubes and nodules) could have been derived from such varied source material and under such widely different local conditions.

But there remain still other difficulties with the prevailing views which, although seldom emphasized today, once sparked a lively opposition to the developing trend of thought. It is worth while to examine those problems thoughtfully, for they strengthen one's conviction that the prevailing theory of the loess cannot be correct as it is. The trail of evidence leads finally to some very startling conclusions, and one

needs the resolve which comes from confidence in his understanding in order to face up to them squarely. We shall
learn about those problems best by attending to some of
that early discussion as it came from the pens of those who
opposed the current views most vigorously. Here, for example,
is how H. H. Howorth argued one point nearly a hundred
years ago [20;p.348]:

> .... the Loess for the most part is completely unstratified.
> Occasionally, especially in America, there are local areas
> where a kind of stratification occurs, but these are very
> local, and I shall return to them presently. This absence of
> stratification I quoted myself as a proof that the Loess is
> neither of marine, lacustrine, nor fluviatile origin [that is,
> neither from seas, lakes nor rivers]. It is assuredly equally
> a proof that it is not due to gradual accumulation by the
> wind. Dunes accumulated by the wind are so easy to study
> that we have no difficulty in finding materials, and assuredly
> they present quite a different structure to Loess. Deposits
> made by wind, especially when made as Baron Richthofen
> suggests, in dry seasons alternating with wet ones, have a
> laminar structure corresponding to the series of layers
> deposited, just as deposits made by water have. Nor should
> we find homogeneous masses several hundred feet thick
> with the same structure and the same contents as the results
> of such a series of seasonal deposits. These masses, to my
> mind, bear, on the contrary, unmistakable evidence in their
> very structure of having been deposited by one great effort,
> and under one set of conditions...

Now here are several interesting observations. For one
thing, Howorth points out that the detailed structure of the
deposit bears no similarity, in general, to sand dunes which
have been blown and redistributed by the wind. From this
one must conclude that the calcite was part of the original
complement of grains which settled down to form the loess;
it was not added afterwards in some unknown way as some
have suggested. Evidently the mass was "frozen" into place
by the calcite the first time that it was moistened by the

rain. The small crystals would dissolve slightly, then grow again as the water evaporated, and in growing anew they would cement the contact between neighboring grains. If the calcite had not been present in the mixture from the very beginning then dune features would have developed while the silt was still free to be moved about by the wind.

Notice also that Howorth objected to the idea of gradual accumulation by the wind. And how could it have been anything but gradual if the silt had been derived from erosion in the Gobi Desert? Erosion, after all, is a very slow and gradual process. Howorth then went on to argue that if the material had been deposited gradually then plants of all kinds would have grown upon it—large plants which would later have been buried in it. But the loess is far different from what one would expect of such an accumulation. As he says above, it bears unmistakable evidence of having been deposited by one great effort and under one set of conditions.

L. S. Berg was another bitter adversary of the prevailing aeolian theory, and he also waged a long fight against it. Here is how this staunch opponent phrased one of his several objections [5;p.134]:

> ... It is absolutely incomprehensible, why the wind should drive sediment of only that texture which is characteristic of loess. The wind, according to its velocity, can carry either coarser or finer particles, but why it should give a preference to particles of 0.01 to 0.05 mm. in diameter, has never been explained by any follower of the aeolian theory. Typical loess being characterized by the predominance of particles of the above mentioned diameter both in Europe, Asia and America, we should have been forced to conclude that the wind had everywhere the same velocity, Moreover, the wind would have to blow in the same direction and with the same velocity during tens of thousands of years. Otherwise the sediment that had settled down could never be so uniform. As in actual fact winds blow with varying force and from varying directions, it is evident that had aeolian loess existed it would have been a mixture of

particles of the greatest variety of coarseness, the texture of loess in neighboring areas at the same time being very diversified...

As one considers Berg's argument with the enormous extent of the loess deposits in mind ("...hundreds of thousands of square miles in little interrupted continuity...") its force becomes irresistible. Even on a small scale the wind has a tendency to mix rather than to sort; how much more likely it is to mix on a large scale! Furthermore, we know very well that the wind carries dust easily and deposits it everywhere, yet these finer particles are notably scarce in the loess.

But problems with the aeolian theory only multiply as one probes deeper, for as it happens gravel and even pebbles are sometimes to be found in the loess! Are pebbles, then, carried on the wind while sand and dust are not? The following description of pebbles in the loess in China is somewhat difficult to follow because the place names are unfamiliar and also the authors gave their measurements both in meters and in feet, but one can hardly fail to get their point nevertheless [43;p.195]:

> Between Ling-shï-hién and P'ing-yang-fu the Huang-t'u [loess] covers the uplands up to more than 1,500 feet, 450 meters, above the river. Underlying strata of the Shan-si coal-measures are exposed in many ravines, but the slopes are buried in fine silt to depths that range from 100 feet, 30 meters, to possibly 300 feet, 90 meters. The deposit is thickest next to the valleys, and is there interbedded with layers of coarse wash. Thus, north of Yön-yi-ssï, at an altitude of 700 feet, 210 meters, above the town, there is a 30-foot, 9-meter, bed of pebbles, up to 5 centimeters in diameter. The bulk of the material appears to be loess, but in sections seen along the road the true constitution is obscured by a coat of dust, and coarser sand and gravels may be present in larger proportions than one expects. Vertical cleavage is everywhere characteristic...

These authors suggested that the coarse material interbedded with the loess, was "wash" because it occurred in layers; they concluded that it had been laid down by running water. But running water quickly carries the loess away, so it could not have been wash in any sense of the word. And of course, the mixture they described could not have been lifted by the wind and carried from some other source.

But easily the most remarkable example of "pebbles" in the loess ever to come to this author's attention was reported by Skertchly and Kingsmill who were also describing a feature of the loess in China. Let us read a portion of their paper, fixing our attention on the "old river gravels" and not being distracted by the perhaps unfamiliar term "Carboniferous" [37;p.243].

> The old river-gravels of Shantung form a very interesting set of deposits... they constitute a conglomerate of limestone-pebbles in a calcareous cement, the component fragments varying from fine gravel-stones to heavy shingle...
>
> The conglomerate is exceedingly hard, and hence has resisted the denudation that swept away the looser material which doubtless originally accompanied it. The beds often stand out as bosses and banks upon the loess-plain, just as, and for similar reasons, many of the ancient gravels of Cambridgeshire and Norfolk rise above the Chalk. So eminently calcareous are they, that in places where no limestone is locally available, as at Chow Ts'un..., they are used for lime-burning. From their very nature they are fragmentary, ranging from 1 or 2 to over 6 feet in thickness, sometimes only a few feet in length, sometimes continuous for hundreds of yards, and from 8 to 30 yards in width. So compact is the mass that fragments 6 or 7 feet wide and 20 to 30 feet long are often seen projecting like shelves from the loess, and at one place we rode through a chasm 15 feet wide spanned by one of these masses hardly a foot thick. It is frequently used as rough building-stone for retaining-walls.
>
> In the great Carboniferous Limestone district which flanks the sacred T'ai Shan range ..., these relics of pre-historic rivers are still to be seen clinging to the valley-sides.

They can be traced at intervals from the hills out onto the loess-plain, and not unfrequently five or six may be seen at different levels on a valley-side. About 80 per cent. of their courses are quite independent of the present drainage-system, and beds sometimes cross each other. Often, too, the roads, which from centuries of traffic have become worn below the surface of the soil, climb laboriously over one side of these old courses, and as abruptly descend on the other,...

In many respects the old river-beds differ widely from those of streams now traversing the same district. The present courses are, where paved with gravel, worn down to the bed-rock, while the old beds frequently lie from 50 to 100 feet above it, the gravel often resting on a level bed of rearranged loess. Then, too, in the recent river-beds, wherever the gravel is made of limestone-pebbles there is no tendency to cement into conglomerate...

Now could those great limey slabs actually be residues of old rivers? One would hardly think so because a river cannot flow upon the loess. Running water quickly wears through the silt and washes it away as the authors were quick to point out in the final paragraph above. Furthermore, they said that 80 per cent of the courses of those "old rivers" were independent of the present drainage system—in other words, the slabs were scattered about at random. Certainly they had nothing whatever to do with old rivers. Here is a problem of heroic proportions indeed, but can it be distinguished from the riddle of the loess itself? Clearly we have only one problem to contend with here, of which the pebbles, the great limey slabs and the silt are merely separate parts, so they must all be accounted for within the same context.

One remaining facet of the problem needs to be considered because it will arise later in another connection. Let us recall that Howorth referred to "a type of stratification" present in the American loess which slightly qualified his argument against seasonal deposition by the wind. This stratum-like appearance can sometimes be noticed in bluffs or where roads have been cut through the loess, and it shows up as changes in color, or changes in the intensity of color, of the material. These bands of color variation are often associated with discernible changes in composition as well.

According to the current view of loess deposition these darker bands constitute "fossil soils", and they are called "paleosols" on that account. That is, each of them is thought to have once been a humus-laden layer upon the surface which formed when the deposition of silt was temporarily interrupted. Of course, the loess is now thought to have been deposited over many thousands of years, and that would allow ample time for such soils to have developed. But if in fact the loess was deposited quickly—"by one great effort, and under one set of conditions", as Howorth insisted, then there would have been no chance whatever for soils to have developed during supposed intermediate stages. It is therefore important to know if those darker bands actually were soils at one time, or whether this is merely a guess having no actual foundation. Here is Berg again, reminding his colleagues what chemical analysis reveals about one aspect of the question [5,p.135]:

> The followers of the aeolian theory affirm that loess is formed not in deserts, whence loess dust is blown off by winds, but on the periphery of deserts, in steppes, where vegetation contributes to the accumulation of loess. Thus, according to this notion, the whole profile of loess had to pass through the stages of soil formation, namely of chernozem, or, at least, of the chestnut type of soils. But in that case a considerable quantity of humus should be present in loess, what, as is well known, does not take place; the content of humus in normal loess is manifested in tenths or hundredths per cent, and sometimes it runs down to naught. One might say that humus had been present once and had subsequently decomposed. But loess beds, as we know, are generally interstratified with one or occasionally several fossil humus horizons in which humus is unaltered; although little humus remains in these ancient

soils, from 0.3 to 1.1 per cent on average, but a humus horizon is always distinct. Thus, if loess had been formed by steppe vegetation being buried under an accumulation of dust, the entire profile of loess should exhibit a semblance of a humus horizon. But such in fact is not the case. Therefore loess could not have been deposited in steppes.

So Berg went along with the idea that the colored bands were fossil soils, but he noted that their actual humus content was very small. He thought that humus had once been plentiful in them but that most of it had washed away during the succeeding years. But might it have been the

PLATE 44: *A view of exposed loess near Council Bluffs, Iowa showing a well-defined layer of soil upon the surface.*

other way around? Plate 44 shows another exposure of the loess at Council Bluffs which plainly shows the sharp contrast between the rich soil layer which has developed at the surface and the natural loess below. One of those darker bands is also evident somewhat below the surface. It is surely significant that the material within this darker band exhibits the typical vertical cleavage just as plainly as does the material above and below. Therefore the tubules are well preserved in this region too so the material could never have been a soil in this sense of the word; its organic component must have some other origin. Perhaps it might be traced most reasonably to the rich soil layer at the top. Some of the soluable humus components there would naturally filter down into the underlying layers, and if the composition of the loess varies slightly in the colored bands then the filtering effect would probably vary also. In that case the colored bands need not have lost a once significant humus content as Berg imagined—more likely those traces which they possess were acquired by seepage and filtration from the soil layer at the surface.

Let us consider those strange tubules again in light of the information which Berg has just given. If they had been formed by grass or other small plants growing upon the material as it accumulated then the organic residues of those plants should still remain, and chemical analysis ought to reveal them as a humus residue, for it is difficult to imagine that such humus could have washed away while the calcite binder still remains intact. Furthermore, if the silt had deposited slowly then larger plants would have grown upon it as well, and their residues also should be found entombed within it. Even if those plants had decomposed entirely, and the organic products of decay had indeed washed completely away, then one should still expect to see the casts of those larger plants preserved as large tubes and holes even as the small tubules are perfectly well preserved. But as a general rule nothing of this kind is found.

THE LOST CITIES OF CIBOLA

Baron Richthofen, we recall, observed that the loess covered the former landscape like a blanket, irrespective of elevation, and he drew the unavoidable conclusion that the silt must have filtered down through the atmosphere from above. That much is undeniably true, but in every other important respect the aeolian theory as it stands today is grievously in error because it fails every test decisively. At this point one ought to be able to declare in perfect confidence that the colored bands are not the residues of former soils, the tubules are not root holes, the silt did not deposit slowly over great periods of time, and finally, and most importantly, it was not picked up by the wind and transported from some former location. One must look elsewhere for understanding, but what are the alternatives?

One interesting possibility was suggested in 1920 by K. Keilhack. He reasoned that if the loess did actually come from the glacial residues, as was commonly thought in the case of the European loess (and still is) then, since those residues contain great quantities of sand in addition to silt, there should also be found residual sand deposits comparable in size to the loess itself. That is, Keilhack looked for the sand which remained after the silt had been removed by the wind, but he did not find it. Therefore he eliminated the glacial residues as a possible source for the silt, and he offered a disquieting alternative in their place. Although his ideas are basically very simple, the following passage is a close translation from the original German so some extra care is required in order to follow his reasoning. Here, then, is the way Keilhack analyzed the problem [25,p.158]:

> ... Calcite and quartz, both important ingredients of the loess, must have been taken by the wind from entirely different places on the earth, for we know of no rock in which they occur together in the proportions and the grain size of the loess since we have had to set aside the glacial formations from consideration. Where, however, and in what way was this astonishingly uniform mixing brought

about as we see it in the loess today—a mixing of these two so different constituents that shows little variation over the whole earth. Can we explain this uniformity in composition in Europe and Asia, in North and South America in any other way than that all the loess masses of these four vast regions have drawn their material from the same large mixing bowl? Must not then the mixing have taken place at a very considerable altitude? The size of the loess particles argues against this, however; they are too large to have remained suspended in the high atmospheric layers for a day, to say nothing of years or hundreds of years. So many questions, so many entirely unresolved riddles!

Starting from the recognition, or the probability, that the entire terrestrial loess is a uniform mixture, and assuming a common reservoir out of which the deposition took place, it is only a step to raise the question whether, in that case, an extra-terrestrial, a cosmical origin for the loess can be entirely excluded? Here, of course, the astronomers have the last word. However, I would not hesitate to suggest it is through such assumptions, bold as they may seem today, that some. of the riddles posed above do find a satisfactory answer,...

But that final word has always come back very clearly in the negative, for according to our customary manner of thinking, the terms "extra-terrestrial" and "cosmical" mean the same thing; they both refer to outer space—the interplanetary realm. And there can be no doubt that if enough material were to fall from outer space upon the earth to form the massive, localized accumulation which prevails in the loess then it would necessarily fall as a meteorite falls, with high velocity and with great energy. The atmosphere would not be able to absorb the energy of such a huge falling mass. From a cosmical encounter on this scale, then, an exceedingly violent explosion would normally be expected where the material struck the earth, and a gigantic crater would be formed with debris piled high around the rim—but of course nothing of the kind is found.

We have hardly begun to probe the depths of the loess, and it becomes ever more obviously a mystery that defies all common understanding—a fitting precedent indeed for those somber hills in Papago Park. It is now clear that the silt did not come from outer space as we understand it, and likewise it cannot be redeposited terrestrial material. Are there any other possibilities?

Perhaps there is one. Our position now might be likened to that of hikers who have encountered a three-way fork in the trail. Two of the paths away have been tested and have proved utterly impassable. Short of turning back only one path remains, but that last way leads over a foggy brink and into a murky darkness which our lights may not pierce. Dare we follow it?

We must!

Chapter 8:

THE THIRD PATH

A S A BRIEF review, let us recall that when we found the Seven Cities we found them dead—and under highly suspicious circumstances. They had been flattened, the inhabitants had been killed, and the heads of their irrigation canals stood high and dry above the badly eroded bed of the river. So little of them remained, in fact, and so confusing were the the signs, that historians were unwilling to recognize them as the same cities that Fray Marcos de Niza had described as flourishing barely a century and a half before.

But the conviction that these were indeed those selfsame cities encouraged us to examine the ruins with a somewhat broader vision than before. Thus were we able to discern residues of an awesome cataclysm in which great quantities of dirt and rock fell upon one large sector of the terrain, burying it underneath. Telltale patterns on all sides, scarcely touched by the passage of years, testified to a bizarre type of phenomenon which caused the rocks to flow inexplicably. Indeed, so incredible was the spectacle that we sought a precedent.

Our studies of the loess have shown that it, too, was born under puzzling and suspicious circumstances. Since it covers the former landscape as a blanket layer there can be no doubt that the silt filtered down through the atmosphere from above. Most who have studied it agree on this point. But current opinion envisions a gradual accumulation of the silt extending over long periods of time, whereas in fact, clear signs show just the opposite; they indicate a rapid deposition as if by one great effort of Nature. More to the point, we found that no plausible source can be cited for the material making up this vast formation. In particular, it could not have been carried by the wind from some previous terrestrial location.

Here also we found signs of the bizarre—of properties that have no accountable origin in terms of the known earth-shaping processes. Only the tragic event at Cibola comes to mind as a plausible similar case, and here the similarity is striking even though the loess differs greatly from the material found in Papago Park. Thus have we gained the precedent we sought, and there can be no denying that it does permit one to view those eerie scenes in the Park with greater confidence than before.

Beyond this, little has yet been gained from our study of the loess which bears directly on the central problem, but if the two incidents were actually similar then progress made towards understanding the one ought to be of help in understanding the other as well. With this hope and expectation in mind, then, let us dig a little deeper into that vast yellow sheet and inquire about the fossils which have been found within it.

From what has been learned so far one might expect the loess to contain very few fossil residues, and at least with respect to vertebrate remains this certainly proves to be the case. Furthermore, again agreeing with expectation, such remains are usually found near the very bottom of the sheet. Evidently the animals were victims of the dust, and they did not long survive after it started to fall. Perhaps we should hear an authority on this important matter, so here is A. L. Lugn discussing that very point [27;p.150]:

The Third Path

Ancient loess deposits contain few vertebrate fossils, and these are found almost exclusively in the lower few feet of any loess, which was deposited at the very beginning of the age of dust-blowing, or in old loess soils at the top of loesses, which were developed during intervals of non-deposition... Apparently, the mammals endured the dust-blowing and the scarcity of water and forage as long as possible; then many of them died and left their bones entombed in the first (lower) few feet of the dust deposit. Those which survived long enough migrated to more hospitable localities, and ultimately the population may have reached quite distant areas. Later generations returned to repopulate the loess areas when conditions again became favorable, and there was forage and water and soil development.

So the normal location of mammalian remains is near the bottom of the sheet as one would expect, but the reason why they are sometimes also associated with the colored bands ("old loess soils at the top of loesses") is not apparent. More commonly, only disjointed parts of plant or mammalian residues are ever found at higher levels in the loess, and these only rarely. But in any case, since we are ignorant of the conditions and the circumstances which brought about the deposition and which prevailed at the time, perhaps we have no firm grounds for anticipating just what might be found within it—or where.

In particular, one would probably not expect to find the shells of snails within the loess, but, as a matter of fact, they abound in it! Indeed, they occur so widely as to constitute a distinctly characteristic feature, and that brings us to one of the most interesting aspects of the entire subject. For while mammalian remains are so rare as to be a genuine curiosity, snail shells occur in great numbers—not everywhere, and not uniformly to be sure, but locally, according to Flint [14;p.253], they have been found in excess of 5,000 to the cubic foot! Moreover, they may be found at all levels, from the bottom of the sheet to the very top!

With only rare exceptions these are the shells of land-dwelling snails, and they usually prove to be of the same varieties as may be found living around and about the deposit today. Plate 45 displays a few such shells taken from the loess at Council Bluffs. The scale is given by the square frame, which is two inches on a side. These particular specimens are not large and neither are they "fossilized"—that is, the original material has not been replaced by silica. In fact,

PLATE 45: *Snail shells from the loess near Council Bluffs, Iowa. Approximately twice natural size.*

one of their most surprising attributes is that they appear to be absolutely fresh and new. Excepting only for their coloration, no degradation is evident even in the most minute of details.

As one can plainly see, these shells constitute a profoundly difficult problem for the prevailing theory of loess deposition since snails require vegetation for forage. If the mammals inhabiting the region were all killed off at the beginning of the "age of dust-blowing", then how is it that the snails seem to have thrived during the whole time? The general absence of any kind of vegetable remains in the loess becomes an even more pressing riddle to the aeolian theory in light of this great army of snails, for if the silt is deemed to have accumulated slowly, burying successive generations of these small animals, then why didn't it also bury the vegetation upon which they fed? As noted earlier, if such plants had ever existed, their organic residues having all decayed away, then hollow casts of their forms should still be preserved along with the capillary tubes, but no sign of any such vegetation is generally to be found. Surely we must now be nearing that fog-shrouded brink, for one can easily sense the visibility becoming shorter. And moreover, the trail has ended. We have arrived at the frontier!

Later on, at our leisure, we shall consider the results of radiocarbon assays which have been made upon specimens taken from the loess. Our interest will also be drawn to the glacial residues in the north and another curious site bordering the silt in Nebraska. However apart from these specific topics we now have upon the table of evidence all the main features of the loess which have been recognized and reported. Many aspects of these now familiar properties have been examined and described in great detail, certainly, but a diligent study of the geological literature on the subject would yield few if any surprises to one who has followed the discussion this far. But those who explored this path before stopped here. Henceforth we must clear our own way.

We need now to account for the snails, and without a doubt the next step forward must be to acknowledge the inescapable fact that they fell right along with the silt itself. The evidence will admit of no other conclusion. And yet for this very reason one might object that, inasmuch as this outlandish conclusion does indeed follow from the evidence as given, then, clearly, since it is manifestly absurd that snails would fall from the sky, it follows that the evidence itself must be faulty, or incomplete in some unknown but essential way. This point needs to be examined at length, so let us pause now to determine if that deduction is in fact of necessity absurd.

Although it is not commonly known, many records exist of unlikely material objects having unaccountably fallen from the sky. Such reports span the globe and extend over the centuries as far back as history is recorded. The phenomenon remains today, as it has always been, an utterly intractable mystery, and this probably accounts for the fact that it is seldom discussed in the literature of the most learned. Even so, a number of writers, sober scientists among them, have carefully collected references to many dozens of such events both from recent sources and from the remote past. Charles Fort was one of the earliest, and he is surely the best known because of his controversial *Book of the Damned,* which was first published in 1919 [15]. In fact, such falls have come to be called "Fortean phenomena" in honor to this crusading author*.

Apparently no hard and fast rules govern these events for they differ widely amongst themselves. Nevertheless, it does usually happen that the falls are confined to a narrowly restricted region, and each incident is characterized by falling

---

* *For a more recent discussion of such incidents see, for example,* Investigating the Unknown, *by Ivan T. Sanderson, Prentice-Hall, 1972— especially Chapter 16 and the extensive catalogue of cases given in Appendix B.*

objects of a single kind—although they may descend in great numbers. As to type, their substance may be animal, vegetable or mineral, and some seem to represent still a fourth category of matter, as yet undefined. As specific examples, one might note that falls in the animal category have included the fleshy parts of mammals, blood (as determined by microscopic analysis), and whole, cold-blooded animals of many kinds both living and dead. In particular, living fishes of various sorts and sizes have been observed to fall on many occasions, as also have snakes, frogs, insects and, yes, even snails!

Now there can be no doubt that this is a genuine phenomenon. Although it does not occur routinely, it has been witnessed many times as the researchers above have amply shown. Nothing would be gained by reproducing a catalogue of such events here, but it will be informative, and perhaps also reassuring, to note two selected cases. The first example is one of the best reported of all because its author was himself a specialist in the study of fish (the falling victims in this case), and he happened to be personally acquainted with many of the eyewitnesses. Let us attend, then, to Dr. Meek's description of this striking incident [27]:

> About 3 o'clock on the afternoon of Saturday, August 24 last [1918], the allotment-holders of a small area in Hendon, a southern suburb of Sunderland, were sheltering in their sheds during a heavy thunder-shower, when they observed that small fish were being rained upon the ground. The fish were precipitated on three adjoining roads and on the allotment-gardens enclosed by the roads; the rain swept them from the roads into the gutters and from the roofs of the sheds into the spouts.
>
> The phenomenon was recorded in the local newspapers, the fish being described as "sile." I was away at the time, but, seeing the account, I wrote to Dr. Harrison, and thanks to him, and especially to Mr. H. S. Wallace, I obtained a sample of the fish, and I was able yesterday (September 5) to visit the place in the company of the latter gentleman.

From those who saw the occurrence we derived full information, which left no doubt as to the genuineness of what had been stated, and this we were able to put to the test, for a further sample was obtained from a rain-barrel which could have got its supply only from the spout of the shed to which it was connected. The precipitation of the fish, we were told, lasted about ten minutes, and the area involved Commercial Road, Canon Cocker Street, the portion of Ashley Street lying between these streets, and the adjoining gardens. The area measured approximately 60 yards by 30 yards, and was thus about one-third of an acre. It is not easy to say how many fish fell, but from the accounts it may be gathered they were numerous; there were apparently several hundreds.

There can be no question, therefore, that at the time stated a large number of small fish were showered over about one-third of an acre during a heavy rain accompanied by thunder; we were informed that no lightning was observed, and that the wind was variable.

All the examples which came into my hands from different parts of the ground and from the rain-barrel prove to be the lesser sand-eel *(Ammodytes tobianus)*. They all, moreover, are about 3 in. in length, or 7.5 cm. to 7.9 cm. they are not "sile", a name usually given to the very small young of the herring. But the sand-eels are sea-fish, and it is evident that the sand-eels showered to the ground at Hendon were derived from the sea.

On sandy beaches around our coasts the lesser sand-eel is very common. As its name implies, it burrows into the sand, but in the bays it may often be seen not far from the surface swimming about in immense shoals—shoals which are characterized by the members being all about the same size.

The place where the sand-eels in question were deposited lies about one-quarter of a mile from the seashore, but it is probable that the minimum distance of transport was at least half a mile.

The only explanation which appears to satisfy the conditions, therefore, is that a shoal of sand-eels was drawn

up by a waterspout which formed in the bay to the southeast of Sunderland, and was carried by an easterly breeze
to Hendon, where the fish were released and deposited. It
is significant that the area of deposition was so restricted,
and that no other area was affected. The origin and the
deposition were therefore local.

We were informed that the fish were all dead, and,
indeed, stiff and hard, when picked up immediately after
the occurrence. This serves to detract from the possibility
of distribution being influenced by such an occurrence, but
it is possible that other species would be able to withstand
such an aerial method of dispersion. It is more than probable that the vortical movement of a waterspout would
transport plankton. This was naturally not observed in this
case, and the small creatures, including eggs and young
stages, would likely be carried over a wider area.

The explanation offered above, that a waterspout had
lifted up a school of fish and later dropped it over the land,
is offered in nearly every such case, but notice that Meek
did not defend the idea very strongly. For not only were
the fish dead when they fell, they were also stiff and hard,
showing that quite a considerable period of time had elapsed
since they had been removed from the water. Furthermore,
they all fell within the narrow space of one-third of an acre,
and they continued falling for ten minutes! Without doubt,
a waterspout would spread its catch over a much broader
area, especially if the fish were held aloft until they had
become stiff and hard. On other occasions fishes have fallen
together in all stages of freshness—alive, and also dead and
putrid, all at the same time.

Here is another example—less precisely reported, but
somewhat closer to our present interest [14]:

When we first heard the report of a shower of snails
having fallen on Thursday week, near Tockington, in this
county, we must confess we suspected the tale to be intended
as a test of our credulity; but the fact has been subsequently authenticated by so many respectable persons, and

having seen from different sources so considerable a number of those little curled light-coloured shells, with a streak of brown, and containing a living fish inside, we feel confident of the truth of the assertion. They fell like a shower of hail, and covered nearly an inch deep, a surface of about three acres, and great numbers were distributed to a much greater extent; shortly after this a storm swept so large a quantity into an adjoining ditch, that they were taken up in shovels-full, and travellers were furnished with what quantity they chose to take, and they were soon carried into the principal towns of this and the surrounding counties!!!

So the prospect of snails falling from the sky may well seem

PLATE 46: *Sawed sections of two typical loess nodules showing interior cracks and cavities.*

absurd to one who confines himself to a laboratory of his own making, but the phenomenon is not unknown to Nature. Ample evidence, then, requires that the snails in the loess fell down from the sky along with the silt—obscure though their ultimate origin may be—and again we have a precedent to lean upon.

As our next step along the way let us recall those limey nodules found in the loess and determine to look inside some of them. Plate 46 shows sawed sections of two typical samples of widely different size and composition. Plate 47 shows another—this one with the end broken off to expose the

PLATE 47: *Loess nodule with one end broken to expose the mud-flat texture of the interior surface.*

interior, and one can hardly fail to notice a surprising common property. That is, they are not solidly filled, and moreover they tend to have a mud-flat texture on the inside. Plate 48 is a close-up view of a portion of the previous sample, and it shows this remarkable feature with unambiguous clarity. Without question, these mud-cracks developed inside the nodule because in its initial, formative state its interior was muddy while its surface was more nearly dry.

Presumably, then, the nodules fell fully formed along with the silt and the snails. The singular wrap-around surface feature of the specimen shown already in Plate 46 supports

PLATE 48: *Close-up view of the exposed interior surface of the sample of Plate 47.*

this conclusion nicely, and the remarkable sample in Plate 49 provides a wealth of evidence which confirms it absolutely. Here the residues of snails are to be seen incorporated within the surface of a nodule from the loess. Notice that none of the shells is intact. In particular, little remains of the one to the left of center, but the residue reveals the unexpected fact that it had been filled with the same material as constitutes the nodule at large!

PLATE 49: *Loess nodule with snail shells firmly incorporated upon the outer surface.*

PLATE 50: *Closer view of one of the shells seen in Plate 49 showing interior filled with nodular material.*

Plate 50 is a closer view of this interesting specimen. It is worth noting that imprints of the cracks in the now-missing shell can be discerned upon the casting which remains. Evidently the shell broke while the "mud" was still soft—that is, very shortly after the nodule had formed. Plate 51 gives a closer look still at the imprint of one of these breaks. The white area at the upper left is, of course, a part of the shell still in place. Notice in this picture that although the mud was sufficiently soft to be disturbed by the breaking shell, a very thin layer at the surface was quite firm—in fact even brittle, since it broke into discrete flakes

PLATE 51: *Close view of the interior casting of snail shell on a loess nodule showing imprint of fracture lines.*

which did not subsequently deform. Then why then did the shell break at all if it was so well supported from behind? Presumably the break was not a consequence of the impact of the muddy ball with the newly fallen silt for the nodule itself, soft as it was inside, shows no evidence of deformation from the impact, and the firmly supported shell should have been stronger yet. Furthermore, once the nodule was in place, buried in the silt, the shell would have been safe from harm. Therefore it seems necessary to conclude that the the shell was filled and the breakage occurred even before it fell to earth.

Plate 52 is a closer view of the coiled shell prominent in Plate 49. Careful examination reveals that it has been squeezed, collapsing in the process—note how the successive coils overlap upon one another. But this is only to be expected in light of our present understanding of the origin of these objects. For the nodule formed as a ball of mud, and the snail became affixed to the surface at that stage. Later on the nodule contracted as it lost its moisture, compressing the shell into its present condition. The surface does not show a mud-crack texture because no tensions developed there in the drying. Tensions would be confined

PLATE 52: *A closer view of the coiled specimen visible in Plate 49 showing deformation due to squeezing.*

to the interior regions where, as previously concluded, the proportion of water was initially greater.

Plate 53 shows another example of loess nodule with residues of a snail affixed: the shell in this case is scarcely imbedded in the surface at all, but instead it mounts upon a kind of pedestal composed of the nodular material which extends out and smoothly into the shell. Plate 54 shows this remarkable feature in greater detail. Note that here again

PLATE 53: *Residues of a snail shell filled with nodular material extending from the surface of a loess nodule.*

PLATE 54: *A closer view of the specimen in Plate 53 showing the pedestal which supports the shell.*

the shell has broken*, and imprints made by the cracked edges of the shell are still to be seen on the surface of the casting. What strange affinity had the mud for the inside of this shell?

At this point we have surely reached the bottom of that foggy pass. Mysteries have added upon mysteries until one can scarcely see his next step; our accustomed lights are of no use whatever. The best that one can do against these puzzles with all of his mundane understanding is to flail about blindly in the dark. But even so we are not lost, for there remains a "guide rope" which will lead us safely along a passable way and out the other side. This rope consists of recognizing that the world to which our eyes have grown accustomed falls far short of the complete whole. The cosmos does not end at our finger tips after all, but somehow, somewhere it continues on. In this context one speaks of an added dimension of space†. It is possible to conceive of such a thing, by analogy at least, but it is not possible to perceive into that other dimension. One need not even try to visualize it. Instead, let us simply take hold of the rope and follow its lead.

Accordingly, on the occasions which we have just been studying, for reasons not yet known, material from another space apparently passed through the black boundary of our

---

* The break in the main body of the shell is natural as before, but the tip was broken by unfortunate accident while photographing it.

† Perhaps it should be emphasized that we are here speaking of a *fourth* space-like *dimension, which is to be sharply distinguished from the now commonly recognized* time-like *fourth dimension. Of course the idea of a fourth space-like dimension is not new; philosophers, scientists and writers have worried the point for many years without ever reaching a firm conclusion as to whether or not it constituted a true property of nature. But here at last is concrete evidence which can be interpreted in no other way. The profound significance of the loess nodules, and especially of those "mud-filled" snail shells, can therefore hardly be overestimated.*

world along this other dimension. Those who witnessed these awesome events, then, watched dumfounded as the rock and the silt materialized out of bare nothingness before their very eyes and dropped gently to the ground!

Now in the two cases of fish falls that were examined, and in nearly every other such instance on record, the phenomenon was closely associated with a thunderstorm and exceptionally heavy rain. One might guess that there was a causal relationship, but little can be gained by seeking understanding in terms of the thunderhead itself for it also is a black mystery which does not yield to present-day physics. The concentration of electric charge which brings forth the lightning bolt simply cannot be accounted for within the framework of normal thought. But now that we recognize spaces beyond our own and allow that material can, on occasion, pass across the boundary into our world, then might one not suspect that electric charge could similarly pass across that black edge?

This is an attractive possibility, for if the electrification of a thunderhead can be accounted for in that manner then its gross behavior can be understood as an easy consequence. That is, it is well known that electric charges of the same kind repel each other. The charges in this case would become attached to atmospheric molecules so that same repulsion would cause the air mass to expand. In doing so it would become less dense, and it would therefore rise. Upon expanding it would also cool, and the cooling would bring forth condensation. Thus one can account for the force which drives a thunderhead churning up into the stratosphere and for the lightning bolt at the same time. Presumably the precipitation of this moisture as rain would be determined by these electrical conditions as well.

One would suppose that this transfer of charge into the atmosphere is governed by factors beyond our earthly plane, and when the normal bounds of these factors are occasionally exceeded then anomalies such as the fall of fish or other animals are observed. Why living animals should be the preferred victims of such quirks is a mystery, and perhaps we need not be concerned with it. But other consequences of these extra-dimensional influences upon our world clearly concern us all very directly. For we have just seen that they probably bring on the rain, at least, and one might guess that they even control the winds that blow. In particular, how could one ever hope to account for the winds of passion —the hurricanes and the tornadoes—in any other way?

Now returning to the loess, those grains of silt must have passed across that black boundary, and by an easy extension of these ideas one can imagine that the particles brought electric charge along with them. If so, then we have a plausible accounting for the very great porosity of the loess and for its tubules as well. For the grains, being electrically charged, would be unwilling to pack together any more closely than was absolutely necessary for physical support; their mutual repulsion would hold them apart. And the capillary tubes could be identified as paths left by the electric sparks which would be expected under those conditions. That is, a flurry of electric sparking would continually dissipate the concentrated charge from the fallen silt into the air above. Then, following the train of thought just outlined, the resulting expansion of the air would force a strong vertical circulation which would carry that charge aloft.

Let us now re-examine those strange nodules found in the loess and see what can be made of them. As already noted, their mud-flat interior leaves hardly any room for doubt about their mode of formation. For it is clear that if the moisture content had been uniform inside and out, and if they had dried slowly, then no cracks at all would form. The presence of mud-cracks on the inside requires that the cores were initially quite muddy while the outer surface acquired additional solids and become dry by comparison. Then, with slow drying, the interior would contract more than the surface, and cracks must form on the inside. But could those additional solids at the surface have been acquired after the mud was in place within the fallen silt? Probably not in significant amounts, because the surface textures visible in Plates 43 and 53 testify that the nodules were already completely formed when they finally came to rest.

The picture, then, must be that the silt and the lime "materialized" in a space which initially contained water globules—not quiescent globules of course, but such as had been disturbed into irregular shapes. While calcite and silt were forming within one of these globules, turning it into a kind of mud, additional powder from its surroundings would come into contact with the surface and adhere. This would give rise to that greater proportion of solids at the surface which is needed to account for the mud-flat texture on the inside. Evidently an occasional snail also came into contact with the globules during this stage, and they also adhered.

Nodular material inside the snails, then, must be traced to the same source—the solids materialized within their bodies and turned them into a mass of mud as well! The volume of this resulting mud would naturally have been greater than the original volume of the small animals themselves, so the excess would have to flow out of the shell as we see in Plate 54. This process could continue until the solids content became so great that the mud would no longer flow; at that point it could only expand in place, and the shell must burst. Therefore one can derive a plausible accounting even for the broken shells, and every shell which this writer has seen embedded in nodules has been broken in this way. Note especially in Plate 54 that where the broken pieces remain in place they do not quite fit. The interior is still too large despite the fact that the mud must have contracted somewhat as it dried.

Thus, up to the limit of that black margin itself, this picture provides a plausible accounting for every observed detail of the loess, its nodules, and its snails, and the vain efforts of the best minds for a hundred years testify that no other alternative exists.

⸺ ◆ ◆ ⸺

How old is the loess? One can hardly imagine that it could be extremely old since both the calcite binding cement which holds the grains together and the snail shells within the mass must dissolve slowly in rain water which seeps down through it. We see a loss of this calcite near the surface, to be sure, but none appears to be missing from within the main body of the deposit. In particular, we have just seen that the finest details of the snail shells show no degradation whatever due to any such loss of calcite.

Radiocarbon assays, on the other hand, would indicate a very considerable age indeed if the laboratory analyses can be interpreted in the usual manner. Ruhe [33], for example, has catalogued a large number of such determinations relating to the loess in Iowa, and a great range of apparent ages is to be found amongst them. In fact, no radiocarbon whatever could be discerned in many samples, and this would normally be taken to indicate an age in excess of 47,000 years. What can be made of such findings?

Clearly, the assays cannot be used to determine age in the customary manner when dealing with samples from the loess, and perhaps the reasons are not hard to find. For one thing, one must know the "initial" radiocarbon content of a specimen —that which prevailed when it was alive—in order to deduce an age from what remains. Perhaps some of the organic materials came across that dark boundary along with the silt and the snails. One has no way of estimating what their initial radiocarbon concentration might have been; in particular, it is not obvious that it should have been the same as in the usual, mundane samples.

But along with the initial concentration, one must also understand the mode and rate of decay of the radiocarbon in order to determine age from the assay. Nothing has ever been found which modifies the rate of decay under normal conditions, but the phenomenon at hand is decidedly not normal. In fact, we now have good and safe grounds for concluding that the loess was deposited quickly, so all samples found within it should be of very nearly the same true age —whatever that age might be. Since the radiocarbon assays turn out differently amongst themselves, one must conclude that the phenomenon itself has distorted the picture. While it continued, perhaps it greatly accelerated the decay of radioactive nuclei in the vicinity*. If so, then this would account for the vast differences actually observed in the radiocarbon concentrations in samples from the loess for presumably such influences would be locally variable.

So the age of the loess remains an unanswered question. Eventually, as the signs are interpreted ever more carefully, its true age may be deduced. In the meantime one can only guess, from the very excellent state of preservation of the snail shells within it, that it must have been deposited comparatively recently—perhaps even within the remote historical period. In this case one might hope to find veiled references to the event in legends which have come down to us from antiquity. But however interesting this subject may be, it is far removed from the present topic, so let us leave it as we found it and proceed along the way.

Brief mention must now be made of the boundaries of the loess. One such region is depicted in Figure 6 which has been carefully redrawn from a figure previously given by A. L. Lugn [24]. However, political boundaries within the state of Nebraska and other details of the original which were not related to the loess have been omitted for the sake

---

* It ought to be noted that the existence of such a phenomenon casts grave suspicion upon all techniques of age determination which are based on the assumed invariability of radioactive decay constants.

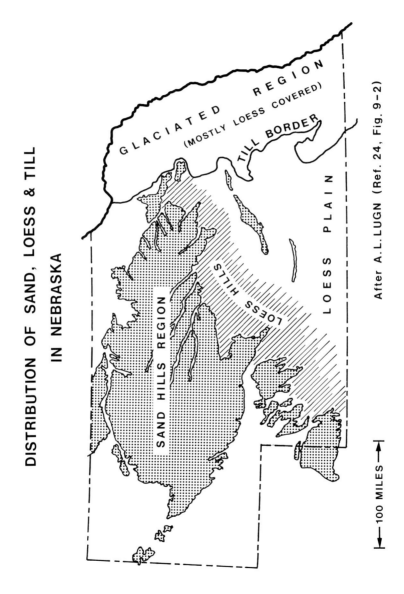

DISTRIBUTION OF SAND, LOESS & TILL
IN NEBRASKA

GLACIATED REGION
(MOSTLY LOESS COVERED)

TILL BORDER

LOESS PLAIN

LOESS HILLS

SAND HILLS REGION

100 MILES

After A.L.LUGN (Ref. 24, Fig. 9-2)

FIGURE 6

of clarity. The Sand Hills shown here are sand dunes which cover an area of about ten thousand square miles, but the sand is now stabilized by a thin layer of topsoil. The sand grades smoothly into loess toward the south and the southeast; the transition region, about 50 miles wide, is indicated in the figure by the diagonal cross-hatching. Here is a sand accumulation of the kind that Keilhack looked for in Europe, but this sand is completely isolated from the till as the figure plainly shows.

The word "till" is used as a verb to denote turning, as of the soil. As a noun it has come to signify soil which has been turned, particularly residues which have been turned or worked by glaciers. The glaciers in question here are, of course, those which are deemed to have spread over the northern reaches of the Earth during the ice ages. One edge of the glaciated region is indicated in the figure, and, as noted, it is here overlain by loess. Without a doubt, the most remarkable feature of these Sand Hills is the shape of their border for as one can plainly see, the Sand Hills occupy a region which is in the shape of a gigantic tear drop! There must be a reason for that. It is as if the sand had materialized within the volume of a great spherical region while the wind was blowing strongly towards the east. The sphere would have been about a hundred miles in diameter, and the sand forms a kind of "shadow", upon the ground below.

Because of the gradual transition between the sand and the loess, one feels strongly that the two materials must have been deposited together. If they had been deposited separately then the junction between the two would have been much more abrupt. Moreover, when one examines the junction between the loess and the till he finds instances where these two grade smoothly into each other as well! Perhaps we should hear eyewitness testimony to this extremely important fact, so here is N. H. Winchell describing one such region in southwestern Minnesota as he observed it a century ago. The term "drift" which this author uses is another name commonly applied to glacial residues. It brings to mind material which has been transported from one locality to another by means of the moving ice [44;p.104].

> The most important fact in connection with the drift of these counties [Rock and Pipestone Counties] is a gradual transition, from north to south, from drift clay, with stones and boulders, to loam clay that has all the characters of the well-known loess-loam of the Missouri valley. The northern part of Pipestone county lies not far from the Coteau du Prairie, which is a vast glacial moraine of drift materials, and is even affected somewhat in its contour by the westward decline of the Coteau to the prairie level. It is as characteristically a hardpan clay—the main mass of the drift, in this part of Pipestone county—as in any part of Minnesota. In traveling southward there is a gradual superficial change in all its characters. This change pervades at first but a small thickness of the deposit but by degrees involves the drift to a depth of 20 feet. At first there is a diminution in the number of visible boulders; then a smoothness in the creek bluffs; then a gravelly clay on the surface, fine and close; then a closeness in the prairie soil; then, in digging wells a few limy concretions [that is, nodules] are seen mingled with small gravelstones, and at last a fine, crumbling loam clay that cannot be distinguished from the loess loam, which extends to Sioux city in Iowa, and there is known as the loess-loam of the Missouri valley and has a thickness of several hundred feet. Wells dug in the southwestern part of Rock county demonstrate also a similar perpendicular transition from loam to drift clay, the former being true loess-loam and the latter true hardpan, or boulder clay. This appears like rank heterodoxy, but it is not a matter of opinion nor theory. It is the result of actual observation. The writer was as much surprised to find it as others will be to read it, and it appears almost inexplicable...

One can easily understand Winchell's consternation and surprise, for the only logical conclusion to be drawn is that the loess and the drift (till) formed together! Now we have been driven to conclude that the loess was deposited very quickly, perhaps even within the space of a few hours, so the till cannot have been left by glaciers operating slowly over tens of thousands of years. These formations leave no doubt in the mind that something very powerful indeed churned up the terrain throughout much of northern Europe, Canada, and the northern part of the United States. Geologists who studied those enormous residues could think of nothing with the majestic power indicated except vast glaciers of continental proportions, and thus were born the "ice ages" which have come to be so familiar. But with our advantage of viewpoint another possibility comes to mind. Might they have been caused instead by that gigantic globe whose shadow we still see in the sand?

Chapter 9:

A FATEFUL RENDEZVOUS

I T IS NOW EVIDENT that the cosmos is much grander than has been formerly imagined. There are spaces beyond our senses and worlds about that we cannot see. It's a humbling realization. How shallow must be our understanding of nature when we perceive only shadows of the whole! What can one honor as wisdom now? How aspire to it? Where seek it?

Although our minds are inherently unable to comprehend this added extension of space, it is possible to formulate simple analogies as an aid to thinking—namely, one can picture two-dimensional "worlds" immersed in a three-dimensional cosmos. For example, a tall apartment building might be looked upon as many two-dimensional realms overlapping upon the same plot of ground, each level being like a world unto itself and going its own way independently of the others. However it's obvious that the various worlds in this building are not truly two-dimensional; they are thin slices in three. And each has two neighbors—one above and one below, so it is separated by two boundaries from adjoining worlds disposed along that "invisible" dimension. Perhaps our domain in three dimensions is analogously a narrow slice in four. We also may be closed in by two such boundaries, though we are not able to perceive either of them, and assuredly we cannot see beyond them.

Although it is vain to speculate about arrangements or details beyond those boundaries, one can at least hope to discern where Nature herself passes through. It has already been noted that atmospheric manifestations associated with the weather are probably brought on by forces from beyond our sphere so one is encouraged to look still further. In fact, it is tempting to guess that the phenomenon of life itself may exercise that fourth dimension in some essential way. At least this thought gives a basis for contemplating such other mysteries as Extra Sensory Perception and the instincts of some of the lower animals. If this is indeed the case then our perception of the biological functions has been embarrassingly naive. How modest our gains after all, and how forlorn the hope of truly understanding these phenomena.

And yet in specific areas there may be hopeful prospects after all. For it seems plausible that the fundamental particles (electrons, protons, and the rest) may be in fact true entities in four dimensions—only their combinations into atoms and molecules being matter in three dimensions as we understand it. In that case their interactions (the "fields" of modern physics) would actually be phenomena in that extended domain. But here our inborn perceptual limitations can be overcome to some extent for this topic is one well suited to a purely mathematical investigation. In other areas, however, the prospects of gratifying insight beyond that dark boundary seem slim indeed.

Let us return now to those enigmatical stone monuments in Papago Park and continue the discussion where we left it. Our understanding will be superficial at best, but perhaps we can now begin to read their grim message nevertheless. Recall that the large-scale flow patterns displayed in Plate 38 seemed altogether inconsistent with melting of the normal kind. The cascading of the rock was frozen in place, and that much lava could never have cooled so quickly. Something other than heat must have caused those rocks to run,

PLATE 55: *A site on McDowell Butte, showing flow features suddenly frozen in place.*

and it was not an isolated case for one can observe that same type of behavior repeatedly in the most surprising circumstances. In some cases, at least, it appears that the caves, which are so characteristic of the buttes in Papago Park, resulted when discrete pockets of rock turned to liquid and flowed away!

Plate 55 shows an example. This site has been seen before from a different viewpoint; it is the second cave up from the "curtained" cave visible in Plate 23. At the left in Plate 55 one can make out the residues of that sheet of melt-rock running down the back wall of the cave, but the

PLATE 56: *A prominent cave in the northwestern region of McDowell Butte which displays the tongue-in-mouth feature.*

structure on the right which appears to be liquid flowing out of the hole is something altogether different. The tongue-like extension from the bottom of the cave continues smoothly back into the cave itself; it has not been "added-on". This material also appears to have flowed very freely, and it too stopped suddenly in mid-flight! In fact, similar features have been met twice before. In Plate 22 one can observe a large flow of rock leaving the cave near the bottom though it is somewhat obscured by the small tree at the edge. Plate 56 is another view of a region shown earlier in Plate 26. Here again the melt seems to be flowing out of the cave, and the

PLATE 57: *Caves in McDowell Butte showing remarkable tongue-in-mouth features.*

combination presents a "tongue-in-mouth" appearance which can be identified at quite a number of sites around the park. Perhaps it should be emphasized that these tongue-like appendages have typically the identical surface structure and rigidity as does the rest of the hill.

Plate 57 displays an especially remarkable example; these caves are situated in a small cleft in the southwestern area of McDowell Butte. The one near the upper center appears to be drooling badly, and the tongue-in-mouth appearance of the one below and to the left is very clear. However it is interesting that the tongue hangs out to the side at a sharp angle and also that the floor of the mouth is correspondingly tilted. Moreover, the drool on the right and the tongue on the left actually intersect, but notice carefully that these two flows did not combine to form a single stream! Somehow they remained separate, for one can clearly discern an isolated but distinct element of the drool well down toward the tip of the tongue.

The enlarged perspective gained from our study of the loess permits an interpretation of these strange features and suggests the probable nature of this melting phenomenon at the same time. Namely, it seems clear that the two fluid streams discernible in Plate 57 flowed independently even though they occupied the same morsel of space as we know it. This suggests that the rocks flowed when they were displaced somewhat—by whatever means—from our worldly space along this other dimension. Then the flow ceased when the material came back "home". Recalling that our world may be closed in by two of those black boundaries, perhaps these masses were simultaneously displaced in opposite directions along that fourth dimension. This is one way in which they could have occupied different spaces altogether while they were fluid so they could flow without merging into a single stream.

As already noted, this tongue-in-mouth feature can be distinguished in a number of caves around the park, but it is by no means common to them all. In light of these considerations perhaps one must regard the "tongueless" caves as the holes which remained when localized portions of the rock were transported along this other dimension and did not return.

Plate 58 gives added insight to the compexity of the phenomenon for here material flows out of the cave as before, but the direction of flow is tilted about 45 degrees from the vertical! One can see the effect best by rotating the page appropriately. Plate 59 shows this feature from a different angle. Portions of the caves seen in Plate 57 can be distin-

PLATE 58: *A shallow cave in McDowell Butte from which rock flowed out at a large angle from the vertical.*

guished just behind it, and Barnes Butte is obvious in the background. Notice that the direction of horizontal defined by the flow in the foreground agrees closely with the level suggested by the bedding features in Barnes Butte, and the slant of McDowell Butte corresponds to this same direction as well. Presumably one must conclude that the direction of gravity was temporarily and sporadically altered during the course of the event.

It is interesting to notice the well defined "seam" where the flow pattern in the foreground meets the rest of the mass on the right. The junction is smooth and orderly, but it is not perfect. This is one of several such explicit junctions which are evident on McDowell Butte, but the topographies on the two sides are not generally so obviously different. Under these circumstances it seems curious that the surface contour should match so well on the two sides.

This might be a good time to recall the unexpected orientation of the icicle-like structures in Echo Canyon Park. Perhaps they also record a locally altered direction of gravity during the time when they were forming; in this context note also the tilt of the tongue in Plate 57.

Plate 60 illustrates another example of this apparent

PLATE 59: *The same feature as in Plate 58 viewed from another quarter. Barnes Butte is visible in the background.*

twisting of the direction of gravity. Here is a view looking east at McDowell Butte from a somewhat closer vantage point than in Plate 25. Judging by the barely discernible ripple-like patterns on the surfaces, these two prominent rock masses also flowed in an unexpected manner, for the motion was far from downhill with respect to our present reference. In fact, the fluid seems to have moved directly across the face of a relatively steep incline, but presumably it moved in accord with the direction of gravity which prevailed locally at the time. Plate 61 is a view looking toward the south at these masses with a segment of McDowell Road being visible

PLATE 60: *McDowell Butte looking east showing large flow features progressing across the incline.*

PLATE 61: *An end view of the flowing rock masses shown in the previous plate looking south.*

in the foreground. Notice that the lower flow is nearly flat, as one would expect of a liquid surface, and this level surface defines a horizontal consistent with that deduced from the forms in Plate 59. With respect to that level, at least, the two masses flowed directly downhill.

Thus far the mind can follow in a hazy sort of way, but no further. But however vague the picture may be in some respects its essential message can hardly be missed— surely this grotesquely twisted mass testifies to an awesome catastrophe of unearthly horror. Worlds folded upon worlds during that paroxysm of Nature, and the cities died. When the fury ended and the dust settled only these silent stones remained to mark their passing. One can now evince little surprise at the divergent results of those radiocarbon assays which so distressed Emil Haury. Perhaps time itself was another victim of the holocaust. Or, as another alternative, possibly the radioactive nuclei decayed more rapidly under those precipitous conditions, their instabilities being multiplied. The assays could not be interpreted in terms of age in either case so at least some of those problems Haury mentioned find a plausible resolution. If the loess fell amid circumstances such as these then we have less cause to be mystified at the great difference in apparent ages of specimens taken from that material also, since, as the forms in Papago Park testify, the effects are subject to substantial local variation.

There seems little prospect of ever understanding the details of that event at Cibola in any meaningful way, but perhaps there is hope of tracing its cause nevertheless. Although most of the patterns seen in the Papago Buttes only compound the mystery, there is one feature which seems clear enough to interpret within the framework of our own world, namely, the apparent association of the hills to a line—a line directed about 20 degrees west of north as seen on the map in Figure 4. This association to a line suggests a path, as if something had moved along it. As a guess, one might suppose that this "something" extended beyond our narrow worldly space and that in passing by it so disrupted the boundary between spaces that foreign material was able to "leak" through into our world. This is merely a hypothesis to be sure, but it is one vague possibility which presents itself for consideration.

It is easy to project a line of reasoning from this point onward because so few options are at hand; one is not obliged to make profound deductions in order to choose from among many alternatives. For as only one interpretation of the alignment of the hills came quickly to mind, likewise we know of only one object—or type of object—which lies beyond our own earthly plane and yet intrudes upon ours. Our sole example is that great globe which we discerned in Nebraska belching forth sand over those thousands of square miles. Here is a type of jigsaw puzzle—not with many pieces, but with only two. If the two pieces fit together then we shall see a picture; if they do not fit then a mistake has been made, and we are finished. Let us try. As one casts his eyes about, looking for something similar to that Nebraska globe, he finds in all of his experience one, and only one, single possibility. A comet!

A comet indeed, whose prime distinguishing features include that great train of dust and sand thrown out to form a tail as it rounds the sun. But if we pay heed to those who have theorized about the nature of comets then we shall be quickly discouraged, because their opinions about these celestial wonders are quite remote from our present needs. However, this may be only because they have never ventured past that foggy brink to gain a view from the other side. Their theories were born in too small a world!

But although their theories may not be valid, at least they give a clear idea of how a comet actually looks to astronomers. Therefore we can see one in that light for ourselves merely by examining those theories briefly. This presents no difficulty for there are only two principal schools of thought, and they are both very easy to understand.

One school conceives of a comet as a great cloud of sand, the individual grains being somewhat separated in space while moving as a group in orbit around the sun. The other school regards one of these objects as a great ball of ice, charged with dirt and sand. According to this point of view, heat from the sun causes the ice to melt and to vaporize, the "steam" thus given off forms a slight wind blowing out from the ball. So the picture is that dust and sand which were freed by the melting are carried away by this wind to be dispersed into space, thus generating the spectacle which we see from afar.

A Fateful Rendezvous

Now the snowball point of view is probably the more appealing of the two because although it has flaws, the problems seem less compelling than with the other theory. For example, if a cloud of sand should pass close to the sun it would vaporize and disappear, yet comets have been observed to pass quite close to the sun with no apparent damage whatever. Accordingly, given only these two options, perhaps it's not surprising that the "dirty snowball" picture should have more proponents than the other.

Champions of the sand bank theory argue that its problems are of a kind which might be resolved as more basic knowledge of comets is acquired, while problems with the snowball theory are said to be so profound as to be insoluble. For one thing, not one of those supposed snowballs has ever been seen—not even with the largest of telescopes. There is sometimes seen a faint localized brightness in the head of a comet called the nucleus, but since this is a transient feature it cannot be said to testify in favor of the snowball theory.

So there are flaws in both pictures, but they tell us everything we need to know nevertheless. They tell us that, to an astronomer having all the greatest instruments at his disposal, a comet looks almost exactly like a great snowball giving forth sand and steam in profusion—but not quite, for no material core has ever been seen. Moreover, we also know that to that same astronomer a comet looks almost exactly like a great cloud of sand having no solid core whatever—but again not quite, because such a cloud must be destroyed on passing close to the sun. But now, combining these two insights, it is easy to conclude that a comet looks precisely like that great globe whose "shadow" we saw in Nebraska. It is an altogether vacant region of space, as far as the eye can see, which gives forth sand in abundance. Why should we not proceed with confidence?

Placing the two pieces of that puzzle together, then, we see a picture of a comet passing close to the earth over central Arizona, disrupting the boundary between spaces and causing the precipitation of the material to be seen today in Papago Park. Likewise, we seem to see the outright collision of a comet with the earth sometime in the more remote past which produced the loess and the till formations.* The object itself apparently came to rest in central Nebraska where it faded away completely after bringing forth that great sandstorm.

Now one might ask whether the supposed comet can be identified which laid waste the Cities of Cibola and gave rise to the hills in Papago Park? Not with certainty, to be sure, for within the living memory of man no comet has ever been observed to strike the earth—not in the time frame of interest here nor in any other. But even in the absence of direct evidence, one can weigh probabilities and arrive at a fairly convincing conclusion, because there is a suggestive clue to point the way. Namely, it is well known that on several occasions comets have been observed to divide into two or more parts, sometimes before the very eyes of astronomers who were watching. At other times, comets passing close to the sun were seen to have divided into several parts, the pieces being strung out along the orbit like the beads of a necklace. The clue, then, is that it is far more likely to encounter a comet in the vicinity of another comet than to meet one at random in space. Such satellite comets would be disposed approximately along the orbit of the main

---

* Perhaps it should be mentioned that Ignatius Donnelly offered this same proposal over a hundred years ago in his book, Ragnarok: the Age of Fire and Gravel, first published in 1883. Although he was necessarily vague about the nature of comets he had studied the drift extensively so he was able to offer many and varied arguments which clearly disproved any kind of glacial origin for it. Having thus eliminated ice in any form, he reasoned that it must have been caused by a comet, this being the only remaining (visible) unknown quantity of Nature which was even remotely plausible. The dubious reader will find Donnelly's arguments both interesting and persuasive.

comet—either leading or following behind.

On the chance that the object of our interest may have been a fragment of some larger comet, it seems reasonable to ask whether the Earth passed through the trail of some known comet during that period—the interval between 1539 and 1694, when the cities were first seen dead. Let us keep in mind that it was only near the end of this interval that the motion of comets came to be understood. In fact, the first comet whose orbit was ever determined was the great comet of 1680, and it was computed by Isaac Newton himself [12;p.334] in collaboration with Edmund Halley. But astronomers had kept records of their observations for many years before that, so our question can be answered in a fairly satisfactory way.

Now it is true that many comets escaped observation altogether in those days; only the brightest of them were ever seen, but the parent of our supposed comet ought to be found among the brighter ones. The dim ones would presumably have been small or more remote and would therefore be less plausible candidates for our present interest. During the interval in question, then, the records show 26 comets which were observed well enough that their paths could be calculated. As records of other observations came to light in succeeding years the calculations were continually refined, and the final results are tabulated today in the Catalogue of Cometary Orbits [25]. An examination of those 26 orbits discloses only two which passed within 1,000,000 miles of the Earth's orbit. In fact, the comet of 1684 passed about 790,000 miles away while the great comet of 1680 passed less than 250,000 miles from the path of the Earth*. Using the radius of the Earth as a unit, these distances are 199 and 62 earth-radii respectively.

So the comet of 1680 is easily the most likely candidate

---

* *This number is defined more precisely in the Appendix.*

to have been the "parent" of the supposed small fragment which passed over Cibola. Not only did its orbit carry it closest to the path of the Earth, but this one was also the largest and therefore perhaps the one most likely to have had fragments associated with it. In fact, by all estimates [12;p.332] that great comet was the most magnificent which the world has ever seen. It passed closest to the Earth's orbit on the 21st of November while it was approaching the sun. However, the Earth did not arrive at that same point until the 22nd of December. The fragment that may have skimmed the Earth, then, would have been following nearly the same orbit, but it trailed along about 31 days behind. As the Earth approached that point, the parent comet continued on its way and soon became invisible in the glare of the sun. It passed behind the sun, emerged from the other side, and became visible again in the evening about the same time that the earth arrived at its fateful rendezvous.

It is an interesting sidelight that while all this was going on, Father Eusebio Kino was awaiting his assignment overseas at the Jesuit College at Cadiz. On the 28th of December (1680) he wrote to the Duchess of Aveiro to give his impressions of this great comet which had then become brightly visible again. Little did he suspect the part that he would play in the drama 14 years later—or that 300 years later we would be reading his mail! But now let us read a portion of the letter he wrote on that occasion and get a firsthand account of that magnificent object [8;p.95]:

... Already [for the 5th day] at six, seven and eight o'clock, we beheld here a huge comet, which I do not doubt was clearly visible in Madrid, but probably disappeared there beyond the horizon an hour earlier than here. On the 23rd of this month, it was first clearly visible to us who are staying in this college; although some had already detected it three or four days earlier.

I have no doubt that this is the same comet which many say they saw before sunrise (between four and five

A.M.) some four or five weeks ago. They beheld it in the east with its nebulous train pointing westward...

That the comet's own motion or lag displacing it from west to east and at the same time diagonally northward was at the rate of almost four degrees daily, I could observe here on the preceding five days, namely on the 23rd, 24th, 25th, 26th, and 27th of this month. Consequently, whereas I calculated that the comet's head on the 24th of this month appeared to us in Cadiz from the occiput of Sagittarius, on the 27th I ascertained that the comet's head had reached the foot of Antinous, so that it seems most likely that in five or six more days it will have ascended to the Dolphin and Aequiculus; and, thus, for several weeks yet, it will enter on a much higher course. We have established that the train of the comet covered some fifty or more degrees, and hence was one of the largest ever seen, extending as it did from the head of Sagittarius to the wing of Cygnus, and hence from the tropic of Capricorn to the tropic of Cancer and beyond...

Both because of its great size, then, and because the Earth passed closest to its orbit, this comet stands alone as the most likely parent of the object which destroyed Cibola and the other communities. But if so, then one's picture of the way a comet would interact with the Earth needs to be refined. For knowing the orbit that it had been following, one can calculate the point in the sky from which it approached the Earth on a collision course, and, as it happens, that point was not visible from Cibola for several hours either before or after the collision should have occurred. And moreover, when it did become visible it was in the wrong direction; an object coming from that quarter would not have traveled the course suggested by the alignment of the hills in Papago Park.

But as a matter of fact, one has no right to insist that the fragment would have merely grazed the Earth and then continued on its way. Another possibility is that it slowed considerably after an initial skimming impact and then proceeded on as if to orbit the Earth. In that case the initial contact need not have been anywhere near Cibola. Figure 7 shows what might be expected after this kind of encounter for three illustrative points of impact around the "edge" of the Earth. Notice that as each of these paths continues, it passes over the site directly opposite to the point in the sky from which the fragment came. All three paths cross at that point.

Now let us suppose that a large pencil had been pressed against the Earth at this "anti-point". All the while the Earth was passing through that zone where the fragment might have hit, the Earth was rotating about its axis, and the pencil would have drawn a line upon the surface. Clearly, that line would be along one of the parallels of latitude, and as it works out in this case that latitude was 22.1 degrees South*.

Let us further suppose that the pencil was wiggled every hour so as to generate timing marks upon the line being drawn. Those marks are shown in Figure 7, and then again in Figure 8. The mark labeled "0" in Figure 8 was drawn at exactly that instant when the Earth passed closest to the orbit of the parent comet*, and the mark labeled "1" was drawn an hour later.

Now if, after the impact the Earth had ceased its rotation, then the subsequent path of the fragment would lie along a great circle—even as a great circle would be drawn upon the Earth's surface. But inasmuch as the Earth did not cease its rotation at that instant, that same behavior would be referenced somewhat differently by a map-maker. The cartographer would show the path veering to the west since the motion of the Earth's surface is itself towards the east. Therefore even if the impact had taken place precisely on schedule the fragment's path would not have crossed the reference latitude (22.1 degrees South) exactly at the 0-mark. If indeed it did progress that far it would have crossed

* *The derivation of these numbers is outlined in the Appendix.*

somewhat to the west, and by an amount which is not strictly calculable from the known data.

The dashed curve in Figure 8 plots the great circle passing through Cibola at an angle of 20° west of north as suggested by the alignment of the hills in Papago Park. Because this circle crosses the reference latitude so very near to the 0-mark one is tempted to conclude that the supposed object passed over Cibola moving in a southerly direction shortly after its initial impact. In that case it had traversed only about 32 degrees of arc across the Earth's surface before arriving at the Seven Cities, so presumably the westward bending discussed above would not have progressed very far. According to this interpretation the impact would have taken place in northwestern Canada (perhaps in the vicinity of 64°N and 130°W) a few minutes earlier than expected.

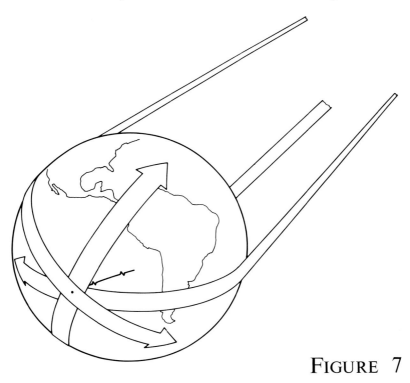

FIGURE 7

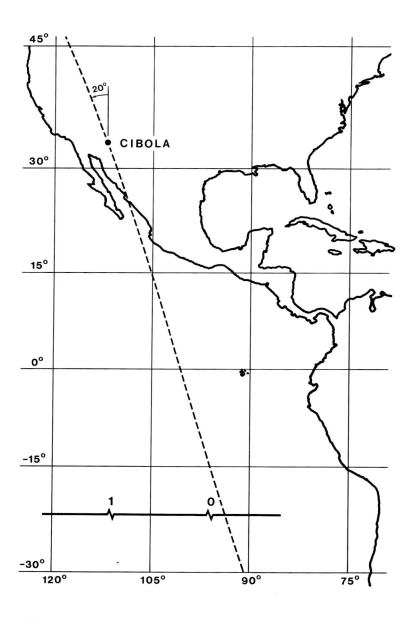

Figure 8

A Fateful Rendezvous

However as one examines Figure 4 (Page 110) again with this aspect of the problem in mind, he must conclude that while the alignment is certainly suggestive, it does not define a specific azimuth with precision. Perhaps the distribution of these little hills was determined only partially by the path of the comet and partly also by the distribution of available source material. In any case the actual time of impact is therefore subject to considerable uncertainty, and in fact, even the direction of motion (whether from north to south or *vice versa*) cannot be decided with confidence from the data at hand.

Of course, some elements of this picture would be altogether inadmissible if the impacting fragment had been a mass of the familiar kind, for one would normally expect an explosive dissipation of energy at the point of impact, and there would be no motion at all beyond. But our hypothetical object is far from familiar, and moreover we have a precedent in that great globe which apparently gave rise to the Sand Hills of Nebraska. It, too, survived the impact and moved about extensively afterwards if we have interpreted the signs correctly. Nevertheless, one's confidence in the picture would certainly be enhanced if independent corroboration could be found for these difficult points, and, in fact, the search for such will be our goal in the next chapter.

Supposing that these problem areas can be supported, then, the cities of Cibola, Totonteac, Marata, Acus and the others met their end in the mid-afternoon of December the 22nd in the year 1680. Would that Coronado and Fray Marcos de Niza had sought the Seven Cities with purer motives so they would not have had to turn away short of their goal. For one must stand in awe before the incalculable consequences of their seemingly harmless deception. If they had continued along their prearranged route then Cibola would have found its place in history, and then also its sudden death would have been a secure fact of record and a challenge to the world of learning for ever after. How much different would have been the development of science and philosophy if that challenge could have been answered! Without a doubt the turning of that army from its planned route there at Culiacán was a turning point as well for the progress of enlightenment throughout the entire world.

Chapter 10:

ISLAND OF MYSTERY

W E HAVE FOUND unmistakable evidence in the loessian deposits that the cosmos extends beyond the range of our senses along a fourth dimension of space. In the previous chapter we found that the current conflicting theories of comets can be reconciled within a single point of view if these celestial wonders are recognized as objects in four dimensions. Their unique properties are then readily provided for, even if they are not explained in detail. Now there can be no doubt that the Cities of Cibola were destroyed by an unworldly cataclysm because the bizarre residues are still plainly in evidence upon the ruins. Therefore it was only a step to identify the root cause of that tragedy as a collision between the Earth and a comet. But we went one step further and made bold to identify the specific comet which might have been to blame.

As the picture now stands, the Earth presumably collided with a small companion to the great comet of 1680—one which followed substantially the same orbit as the latter but which trailed along behind by some 31 days. In that case the encounter must have been very much different than would have been a collision with, say, a small asteroid. Instead of coming to rest at the point of impact, or perhaps even disintegrating completely in an explosive dissipation of energy, the object must have survived largely intact and continued to move as if in a low orbit near the surface of the Earth. If this was indeed the comet which destroyed Cibola then the path that it should have traced upon the Earth is defined, at least approximately, by astronomical data. Certainly the next step is to look for telltale signs along this course.

Even just a cursory inspection of the region to the north and northwest from Cibola reveals many terrain features which might have stemmed from an event of this kind. In fact they are so common that they cloud the issue, for they

PLATE 62: *A small hill of powdered gypsum with congealed pools of rock scattered over the surface.*

are not strictly confined to a well-defined path. Very tempting sites showing clear evidence of bizarre origin are to be found scattered over a disconcertingly broad region extending both to the east and west of the dashed curve in Figure 8. Plate 62 shows one example. This is an isolated hill of powdered gypsum, maybe four or five acres in extent, situated in northwestern Arizona a few miles east of Hoover Dam and about 75 miles west of the expected path. Upon the surface of the gypsum are scattered small "pools" of once-molten rock, one of which is shown in Plate 63. These little pools vary greatly in size and color, ranging from nearly white to

PLATE 63: *Sample of a congealed pool of rock from the gypsum hill of Plate 62.*

almost black and from a few inches to perhaps a yard across. Oddly enough, they seem to have formed and congealed before having fallen into place. The deposition appears to have been very recent for one can observe in Plate 62 that the congealed pools, where undisturbed, protected the gypsum underneath from dissolution by the rain, and therefore they stand on little pedestals about three inches high.

According to the present point of view the comet was not itself the actual source of the gypsum and pooled rock, nor do these give any hint of having impinged with significant horizontal velocity. Instead, the comet seems to have somehow disrupted the boundary between spaces in passing and, acting as a kind of "funnel", permitted the alien material to leak into our world along that fourth dimension. Thus one can understand in a general way why residues of the passing might be distributed sporadically and show wide variations in character and composition from one site to another.

The above is but one of many interesting examples which might be offered as evidence for the phenomenon in a general sense, but owing to their broad geographical distribution they cannot be said to support this particular picture very well. Of course, one has no way of knowing how wide the region of interaction might have been. Perhaps it was very wide indeed. And also there may have been other events of this kind in the not too distant past. Since the region is quite arid weathering is slow, so the residues might continue to appear fresh for a very long time. Clearly, then, the ideal site for study would be one far removed from Cibola so that the width of the interacting region would be less of a confusing factor, and moreover, one would hope for a site which could be dated independently.

And perhaps we have it. A small island in the south Pacific with a strangely puzzling background presents itself for serious consideration. It was first discovered for the western world by Jacob Roggeveen, a Dutch sea captain, on Easter Sunday of 1722, and he dubbed it Easter Island on that account. Roggeveen landed a party to investigate the new spot, and he noted many huge statues standing round about. His first reaction was to marvel that those primitive people could have erected such great monuments with no heavy timbers or cordage at hand, but upon superficial examination he concluded that the statues were modeled in clay. Actually, they were carved in stone at a remote quarry and were moved over rudimentary paths to their stations. Those enormous statues—and especially the mode of transporting them—constitute a profound riddle which has mystified the entire world. Apparently at least part of the problem can be traced to the comet, so let us review the present picture in some detail.

Unfortunately factual information from those ancient times is very scarce, because more than a century passed after the time of Roggeveen before serious effort was made to reconstruct the history of the island and discover the meaning of the monuments. By then it was too late to obtain definite information because several tragic circumstances combined to confuse the people's links with their past. For one thing, Peruvian slavers raided the island around 1860 and took those who were most learned in the ancient traditions to work the guano deposits of the Chincha Islands. To make matters worse, the natives at that time were constantly engaged in savage inter-clan wars which further decreased the population and degraded their ancient ties. Negotiations with Peru eventually caused a few of those slaves to be returned, but the latter brought smallpox back to the island so the population was reduced even more. Thus did the past become ever more cloudy so that only a few vague shadows remain today.

Easter Island was formed from the outpourings of three main volcanos, one of which provided the material for those great statues. This one is called Rano Raraku, and its walls are of a fine-grained tuff very suitable for carving. Plate 64 shows a few of the statues—called moai by the natives—

PLATE 64: *A few of Easter Island's giant statues standing on the slope of the quarry volcano Rano Raraku.*

standing on the slope of Rano Raraku. These were still in the finishing stages and had not yet been taken to a site for permanent mounting. Those which had been established at permanent sites were, without exception, deliberately toppled over during the inter-clan strife.

Plate 65 shows a group of eight moai in their present vandalized condition. Usually the tipping was carefully arranged so that the heads broke off when they fell. Perhaps these will some day be restored to their original place as has been the example in Plate 66, which is a photograph made on the occasion of its restoration. The majestic size of this one is made clearly evident by the crowd of people

PLATE 65: *A group of vandalized statues toppled over onto their faces, most with their heads broken off.*

PLATE 66: *A giant statue with top-knot as restored to place in modern times.* PARIS MATCH Photo-Saulnier.

standing before it. Note that it wears a hat, as many of them did. These top-knots, as they are called, were carved at another site entirely and were balanced upon the heads of statues after the latter were finally in place upon their altar-like foundations. About six hundred of the statues were carved in all. They differed in size and in minor detail, but with only one exception they all seem to have been fashioned after the same model.

Modern attempts to explain the mode of transport of these massive statues have all taken for granted that the large timbers which would have been needed for levers,

PLATE 67: *Model of an ancient boat-house. Photographed in the Father Sebastian Englert Museum on Easter Island.*

rollers and derricks were readily at hand. But all signs indicate that the island was devoid of large plants in those days. There were certainly none when Roggeveen visited, and indeed the very life style of the ancient people testifies to the absence of load-bearing wood even from the earliest times. Plate 67 illustrates one common form of house from that period—called a "boat-house" today because of its characteristic shape. To some extent this is a conceptual model because nothing remains of the original structures, but many foundations survive so there can be no doubt about the general form. One of these foundations is shown in Plate 68.

PLATE 68: *Original foundation stones of an ancient boat-house not far from the statue shown in Plate 66.*

Island of Mystery

It consists of a number of easily manageable stones, shaped and fitted end to end, with socket holes drilled at intervals to receive the rib-like elements, which may have been bamboo. Natural caves walled in with rocks were also utilized where available. It is scarcely possible to imagine that a people with the vision to conceive and execute those grand monuments would have lived in such cramped primitive quarters unless they were compelled to do so—king and drudge alike—by ultimate necessity. Nowhere on the island is there any direct evidence whatever for the ancient use of structural wood or strong cordage.

But the statues are only part of the riddle; the other part concerns the people who produced them. For it appears that some sudden, long-forgotten tragedy effectively destroyed the statue-building culture sometime during the latter half of the 17th century. One cannot fail to notice that this includes the time of the comet so the nature of that tragedy is a matter of special interest. As already noted the past is very dim here, but careful studies have recovered the following basic information:

In the olden days Easter Island was populated by two races of people who came to be called the "Slender People" (Hanau Momoko) and the "Stout People" (Hanau Eepe)*. The Slender People arrived first, coming by canoe from an unidentifiable land called "Hiva", and their leader became the first king in the royal line. The actual date of that landing is not known, of course, but it seems to have occurred at least several centuries before the time of the comet. The Stout People came sometime afterwards; they were men only so they took wives for themselves from the other tribe. These Stout People were a minority, but they appear to have been somewhat more clever than the others because they soon came to be the foremen and effective rulers of the island.

---

* *The older interpretation of these names as* Short Ears *and* Long Ears *is erroneous according to some modern authorities.*

THE LOST CITIES OF CIBOLA

As it happened, the King occupied a most unusual position in the community; in fact he hardly ruled at all in the normal sense. Custom has it that members of the direct royal line possessed a certain power called "mana" which worked for the general good of the people. Whatever may have been the basis for this idea, it was the foundation for the entire culture. According to the natives it was an entirely impersonal power which had its seat within the king's head. As a consequence of this belief, the skulls of past kings were sometimes stolen from their graves in hope that whatever mana remained might work locally to the advantage of the thief or his clan. The King's only duties, then, were to preside over certain ceremonies and to propagate the kingly line so this mana could be preserved in his first-born son.

Years ago, when the natives were first asked how the statues had been moved from the quarries to other parts of the island their invariable reply was that they moved, in effect, all by themselves by means of the mana. They explained that mana no longer existed on the island—that it died with the last king of the line in about 1870. But the statues had stopped long before. In fact, most had already been tipped over by that time, and they could not be righted again.

The quarry mountain, Rano Raraku, constitutes a kind of "window" looking out upon those former times. Through it one can easily discern that a great many workman took part in carving the monuments, and it is equally clear that work stopped suddenly, as if in a single day. In fact more than two hundred of the partially made statues are still to be seen there, some very nearly finished while others were only just begun. Even those which were in transport along the way stood fast and moved no further. If work had trailed off deliberately then certainly the inventory of statues in progress would have been smaller or even altogether nil.

It is worth noting here as an aside that despite this sudden and unexpected work stoppage, with many statues stopped in transport, no trace of any transporting apparatus survives—either along the wayside or upon the quarry mountain. Furthermore, statues had been carved—and were being carved both inside and outside of the volcanic cone at sites accessible only with a sure foot, and even there are to be found no ramps or engineering emplacements, nor any sign that such ever existed.

Tradition accounts for the work stoppage in this way [11;p.130]: Upon an occasion, the Stout People ordered the Slender People to pick up all the stones on the island and throw them into the sea. The Slender People, not wishing to be ordered about any longer, rebelled, and the decisive battle took place at a kind of trench, called the Poike Ditch, which separated their respective domains. The Stout People, having got wind of the rebellion, retreated behind this trench and threw all kinds of burnable debris into it; their plan was to ignite it while the Slender People were crossing the ditch to attack them. However, by a ruse the Slender People turned the tables and threw the Stout People into the burning ditch instead. Only one lone man from among the Hanau Eepe was permitted to survive—that he might have descendents.

Father Sebastian Englert, for a long time a priest on the island and a student of the native traditions, was able to determine the approximate date of the rebellion by a careful study of that man's progeny. More exactly, he placed the birth of that lone survivor somewhere in the latter half of the 17th century [11;p.134]. This is only approximate, of course, but it is significant because other evidence points to that same time period. In particular, excavations in the Poike Ditch were later carried out by a Norwegian expedition under Thor Heyerdahl, and a charcoal sample was taken from what appeared to be the remains of a great fire. Carlyle Smith interpreted the subsequent radiocarbon assay in these words [39;p.391]:

> This leads to a slight reinterpretation of the legend. The Hanau Eepe may have retreated behind an existing fortification which had been constructed many generations

earlier to meet just such an emergency. Our investigations support the legend to the extent that the ditch and mound are undoubtedly man-made, and that a great fire burned in the ditch. No traces of burned human bones were found, but when the length of the ditch is considered the chances of finding such remains were remote.

The date of *ca.* 1680, for the great fire, and the absence of the *mataa,* or obsidian spear head used in warfare, suggest that the war between the Hanau Eepe and the Hanau Momoko marked the end of the Middle Period, when the *mataa* seems to have been unknown or rare, and the beginning of the Late Period when it was common.

Now this radiocarbon date is only deemed accurate to within a hundred years so this exact agreement with expectation is fortuitous; nevertheless it is certainly reassuring. Evidently that profound change in the social structure took place at about the time of the comet, and several strong clues indicate that there was a direct connection between the two events.

The first is a provocative legend from ancient times recorded by Maziere [26;p.57] which goes like this:

> In the days of Rokoroko He Tau the sky fell.
> Fell from above on to the earth.
> The people cried out, "the sky has fallen
>   in the days of King Rokoroko He Tau."
> He took hold: he waited a given time. The sky
>   returned; it went away and it stayed up there...

This is a remarkable statement. Otherwise wholly devoid of meaning, it is most apt indeed in light of what we now know about matter falling from the sky, stimulated by the close passage of a comet. But there are minor complications.

It happens that there were two of the royal family who bore that name, but only one was actually a king. This one was next to last in the line of succession, and he died as a boy of tuberculosis in the year 1867. The earlier one was a son of a previous king, but he was not heir to the throne so it is necessary to interpret the legend slightly. To this end let us hear Métraux tell about that former Rokoroko He Tau. This noted French authority on Easter Island is here discussing the power of mana [31;p.90]:

> This power over nature was concentrated in the eldest son; but sometimes it developed such intensity that it risked becoming the source of numberless evils. The legend of the little prince Rokorokohetau, son of the third wife of King Nga'ara, affords a famous example of this. The case is particularly curious because this king's son had, by birth, no right to royal dignity. His entry into the world was accompanied by wonders such as generally announced the birth of a great chief. Many people were devoured by sharks, and sea beasts appeared on the shore and attacked those who ventured there. Finally, white fowl—hitherto unknown—began to multiply. These miraculous events were manifestations of Rokorokohetau's mana. In the hope of averting these disasters and saving his people, the reigning king had his son taken away and shut up in a cave on Mount Rano-aroi. In vain—because his subjects, convinced of the sanctity of the little chief "with the diadem of white feathers", refused to carry before the legitimate heir the standards symbolic of royalty. In the end Nga'ara had his son, whose mystic power had such baleful effects, put to death.

These remarks are worthy of considerable attention, but for the present* let us be content to observe that although this prince was not in line for the throne, nevertheless, owing to the highly unusual circumstances many of the people acknowledged him as king. Therefore the legend could very well have reference to this one, but the list of kingly successions as reconstructed in modern times poses a more serious problem. For King Nga'ara, the father of that controversial prince, is given there as only the third before the legitimate King Rokoroko He Tau. If this is actually correct then it would not be possible to associate the comet with that reference to the falling sky; the three reigns would have to

---

* *Some additional observations are offered in the Epilogue.*

span nearly two hundred years. But let us take those dark days in the last century into account and acknowledge that there may have been gaps, probably not it the royal line itself but at least in the names which survived.

In that case the legend of the falling sky deserves further attention, so with it in mind let us reconsider that strange order of the Stout People—to pick up all the stones on the island and throw them into the sea. This is hardly credible as it stands because Easter Island is exceedingly rocky. Indeed, it's not much of an exaggeration to say that there would be little left of it if its stones were all thrown into the sea. But a few specific stones are notable because they are decidedly alien—not of volcanic origin at all. These are small, smoothly rounded pebbles, somewhat flattened, typically about two inches across, and they are all to be found on the "front porch" of the Ahu Akivi. Plate 69 is an attempt to display these alien stones in place. The large rounded rocks are of local volcanic origin and are typical of all the Ahu, but the small stones between the latter, only barely distinguishable in the photograph, are unique to this one.

This multitude of foreign stones, all collected at this one imposing spot, suggests that the legend became somewhat distorted during those bad years. Possibly the original phrasing went something like this: Upon an occasion, the Stout People ordered the Slender People to pick up all the *newly fallen* stones on the island and throw them into the sea, *but the Slender People insisted upon offering them to the gods instead.* In that case the conflict which followed was a religious war, often the most brutal kind of all.

We have seen the next clue already in Plate 64; the giant statues standing on the slope of the quarry mountain Rano Raraku have been buried under upwards of ten feet of earth and debris! Only the heads of those huge statues are to be seen protruding through the overlying mantle. Commentators have come to refer to this material as "rubble" because they suppose it to be ejecta from the quarries—that

PLATE 69: *The Ahu Akivi with its seven restored moai and a multitude of alien pebbles barely visible on the front porch.*

is, the carvers' chips, but its volume is unquestionably many times greater than that of all the quarry holes combined. Plate 70 is a view from afar of the base of Rano Raraku showing the wide extent of this dirt deposit, and in order to gain still more feeling for its size and appearance let us attend to Arne Skjölsvold, a member of the Heyerdahl expedition, as he describes it in his own words [38;p.342]:

> The most convincing evidence of the extent of the industry in Rano Raraku in ancient times is found on the outer edge of the southern part of **the** mountain. Here are long and impressive piles of grass-covered quarry rubble

PLATE 70: *Showing the extensive piles of earth and its buried statues at Rano Raraku. Note the enormous unfinished moai in the background rock just to the right of center.*

along the side and foot of the mountain. It was immediately apparent that these characteristic features in the local terrain were not natural formations, but the work of men. Scattered upon and between these earthworks are about fifty gigantic stone statues, most of them buried up to the neck in earth and rubble...

There are good reasons for believing that quite a large number of statues are hidden below the surface. This applies particularly to the area at the foot of Rano Raraku, where enormous quantities of rubble from the quarries probably cover a large number. Both our own and Routledge's excavations have shown that there are good reasons for such an assumption.

He goes on to give a few measurements of these mounds and then he concludes as follows:

> It is impossible to visualize how the volcano looked originally. The quarrying activity and the enormous quantity of rubble have completely altered the local topography.

Notice that the writer describes this material as "earth and rubble"; later on he gave more details. The various textures noted in the wall of their exploration trench were indicated on a diagram, and distributed irregularly (not in order from

PLATE 71: *Giant statues buried in the rubble at Rano Raraku showing pronounced tilting.*

top to bottom) were regions described as:

> Black soil, stone picks, much stone debris
> Light sandy soil, stone picks, much stone debris
> Sandy soil, clay, stone debris, stone picks
> Black soil, clay, stone debris, stone picks
> Coarse stone debris
> Etc.

Assuredly there was much stone debris left over from the carving operations, and presumably it was disposed of somewhere in the vicinity. But the black soil, the light soil and the clay mentioned here are decidedly alien, and they must account for most of the enormous volume of this deposit. One can only feel a sense of relief that he has means at hand to account for both the foreign material and the mixing. The comet, to be sure.

Apparently this was a scene of tornado-like fury, for note in Plate 64, and also in Plate 71, that during the process of being buried many of the statues were also tilted. In fact, without the accumulating debris for support they would have fallen over. One would not think to trace this tilting to the vandalism of later years because if great force had been applied after they were already buried then the heads would have broken off. It is interesting to note in Plate 70 that traces of the deposit are to be seen even at the very top of the mountain.

As a new point on the path, Easter Island is easily consistent with expectations. One can now estimate that the comet fragment followed approximately the course given by the solid curve in Figure 9—although the direction of motion still remains undetermined.

On that fateful day of the comet the Cities of Cibola passed into oblivion, their cries of anguish lost in the wilderness. There was none to tell their story because no survivors ever reached the Spanish domain where an account could have been preserved. Some might have made their way to

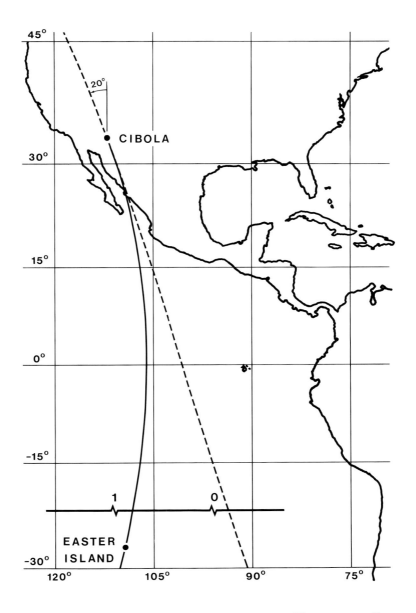

FIGURE 9

New Mexico, to be sure, but recall that only four short months previously every white man in that vast region had either been killed or driven out; not one penman remained to make a permanent record.

This seems the saddest part of all because although those cities never acquired the technological trappings of the European nations, they surpassed the latter in other qualities of a civilized community. For they had the wisdom and the humanity to live together in peace*, during fat times and lean, for multiplied centuries. And according the the description left by Fray Marcos they were an industrious, refined and intelligent people who were admired and respected by their neighbors. One feels the tragedy all the more keenly that such an exemplary nation should have passed unmourned, for, truly, to die unmourned is to die indeed.

---

* In this context let us recall that the elderly Indian whom Fray Marcos described in Paragraph 13 of his account mentioned a war between Marata and Cibola. However modern archaeologists have found no evidence whatever of Hohokam battlefields and, for that matter, only rare evidence of physical violence of any kind. It would seem that the conflict that gentleman spoke of could not have been much of a war by the white man's standards.

Epilogue

A FTERTHOUGHTS

IN MANY respects I find the fruits of these explorations to be immensely gratifying since they give a broad new insight to Nature and her workings, but in other ways they are just the opposite. For we have watched extensive areas of interest slip away into the imponderable leaving faint hope for satisfactory understanding there. Perhaps among these is the most compelling of all—the vast mystery of life and its processes. If, as now seems plausible, the latter are not confined to three dimensions then I fear that they can never be mastered in any meaningful way. Formerly the imponderable mysteries could be set aside in a category by themselves to be ignored if desired, but now the bizarre has to be acknowledged even in areas claimed by the exact sciences. Without a doubt this new insight has complex implications, but I gladly leave to others the task of analyzing them. Only a few brief observations and speculations do I presume to offer.

In the beginning of Chapter 9 I observed that the fundamental particles might be entities in four dimensions, only their combinations into atoms and molecules being matter as we understand it. Here I might add that in this light one can easily understand the peculiar wave-particle duality which gives rise to their so-called quantum mechanical behavior. For though they may be objects in four dimensions we are constrained to observe them in only three; that is, we see them only as a three-dimensional projection. Therefore, depending upon the mode of projection, the observed properties might be variable, but they must always be properties agreeable to a three-dimensional space. Thus in one manner of projection they appear simply as particles; in another purely as waves, but they can never manifest themselves as both wave and particle at the same time because (as it happens) there is no such thing as a "wave-icle" in three dimensions. One can anticipate that this "projection problem" might lead to complications when observing any four-dimensional entity or process whatever.

I also noted that the interactions between fundamental particles were likely to be processes in four dimensions. Our study of comets supports this conclusion and leads naturally to another one which may be of interest. For comets, as we recall, show every sign of being macroscopic objects in four dimensions and yet, apart from a specific class of very small deviations, they obey the same law of motion and even experience the same gravitational potentials as do material bodies of the normal kind.

But if the gravitating mass of comets actually lies outside of our "plane", while interacting with bodies within it, then the gravitational interaction must be of a four-dimensional nature as well. It has been seen that in some sense we are overlaid by other worlds—the source of the material which has leaked through into ours on occasion. Then the question naturally comes to mind: How much of the Earth's observed gravitational field arises from mass that we can see, and how much stems from those other worlds which we cannot see? Now we know very well that the gravitating mass of the Earth is much greater than could result from a purely rocky composition throughout. The "extra mass" is thought to reside in a dense metallic core, but now one can discern another possibility. Perhaps it lies beyond our plane altogether, being a manifestation of those other worlds.

Afterthoughts

This may seem fanciful at first so for the sake of completeness I would like to defend the idea briefly by taking note of the observed rate of precession of the equinoxes. (Those who are not familiar with this problem might prefer to skip these remarks altogether.) It is well known that the equinoxes precess in response to the action of the sun and the moon on the equatorial bulge of the Earth and that the rate to be expected is precisely calculable in terms of certain ratios of the Earth's principal moments of inertia. It is therefore independent of the actual mass of the Earth and depends only on the relative distribution of mass. Surprisingly enough, the observed precession rate agrees almost exactly with the rate to be expected of a uniformly dense spheroid having the external form of the Earth. So there is no hint here of any dense metallic core. And if such a dense core did exist it would have too small of an equatorial bulge of its own to contribute its fair share to the torque giving rise to the precession. This deficiency, in turn, would generate a substantial relative motion between the mantle and the molten core which would have discernible external effects. But no such effects are actually observed so apparently there is no dense core after all. In that case the extra mass must indeed belong to those other worlds.

We saw in Chapter 8 that the loess with its snails entered our world along that fourth dimension. It seems evident that a great many long-standing mysteries can be resolved by recourse to this same kind of process or phenomenon. Most immediately to mind comes the riddle of the frozen mammoths of Siberia. Not only are these huge animals found frozen in the tundra with residues of tropical plants still identifiable inside them, but their interior parts were preserved by freezing before decay could set in. Evidently their bodily heat was lost, not slowly by conduction to the colder surroundings, but immediately as part of their bizarre transition. The fossiliferous rocks are a similar case in point. It is interesting that species found in the rocks are sometimes to be found living on the Earth today so evidently that transition process admits of variations, some of which are not even fatal to living organisms. In that case one can't help but wonder how much of life on Earth had its origin in events of this kind.

It is only a small step to note that our new-found phenomenon gives an obvious basis for the universal flood mentioned in the Bible and other ancient writings. In former times the widely prevalent fossiliferous rocks were regarded as clear proof of such a flood, but then more recent geological theories ascribed a much different origin to them. Now we perceive still another one; the substance of the rocks and their burden of fossils are probably alien to the Earth alto-gether. However, catastrophic flooding is an easily conceivable consequence of the type of event which likely gave rise to them, so the Biblical account deserves careful reconsideration. One important and probably very difficult task will be to deduce dates for these events, for certainly the present schemes for dating rocks can no longer be admitted. Another point to be noted is that the Scriptural flood was said to have been caused by a deliberate act of God, whereas our experience is with supposed consequences of cometary encounters. However, the account goes on to state that God gave Noah 120 years' advance warning of the catastrophe—as if it were to be a natural event of which He possessed supernatural foreknowledge.

Sometimes I think that I discern a similar foreknowledge of the event in our case—dimly to be sure, but I'll share the view as a closing thought so the reader can appraise it for himself at his leisure. To this end, let us return to Easter Island and contemplate the riddle of those strange statues one more time.

In the text I went to some length to explain how profound is the problem of accounting for the transport of those great masses. For it was evident from the living accommodations of the ancient Islanders that they possessed no load-bearing wood. I could have gone further and described the ancient housing at a site called Orongo on the southwestern tip of the island. It consists of shelters made of flagstones laid like bricks without mortar. The rooms are long, but so narrow as to be topped by a single flag of a size manageable by one or two men. Were these the largest flagstones available? I don't know, but it hardly matters. They had a quarry from which they could have carved stone rafters of any size and length, but they did not. So the plain evidence requires a further surprising conclusion. Not only did the Islanders possess no load-bearing wood, but they were also unable to move heavy stones!

The question now is whether reason or prejudice will prevail, for reason clearly requires that the Islanders could not have moved the statues by any customary means whatever. The statues can only have moved by the power of mana, as native tradition has maintained from the very beginning.

But if mana could move the statues why couldn't it have moved stone rafters and other needed structural elements just as well? Probably it could have, but from the fact that it did not one must conclude that the King had no control over it. It must have been managed by some other intelligence—certainly more than human—which pursued an end of its own. Evidently the immediate purpose was to produce the statues and place them around the island.

In that case everything about the statues may be of significance, but for the present let us be content to note that while they were made in a great range of sizes they were very similar in other respects—even to their facial expression. Perhaps this indicates that they were meant to be a group with a common spirit and not merely a random crowd. This idea is strengthened by the fact that they all faced inland; so they were a circle—a group with a common intent.

Now let us consider again that great social turmoil at the time of Prince Rokoroko He Tau which Métraux spoke of. We recall that the people refused to carry before the rightful King the standards appropriate to the royal dignity. Clearly this was not because the young prince had such great manic power as Métraux suggested, for in fact he had none at all. The reason can only have been the failure of the King's own power. Obviously the statues quit moving on some occasion, and this must have been the time. No doubt this is the reason work stopped at the quarry; there was no point in carving on the statues if they would not move when finished. And this also accounts for the importance attached to those alien stones; perhaps the Stout People felt that they were somehow poisoning the mana and that the power would return if the island could be rid of them altogether.

So the statues quit moving upon the occasion of the comet; apparently they were now to play their assigned part. As a clue to what that part might have been let us note the expression upon their faces. Their lips protrude—the universal appearance of one holding back the tears. But is it universal? As a check I asked some of the Easter Island natives what emotion they read upon the faces of the moai. Without revealing my purpose I inquired of six as opportunity permitted. Of these, two answered "deep thought"; two more "sadness"; another "sorrow", and the sixth "anguish". So I am not alone in perceiving that the statues were expressing grief. In that case their role was a poignant one. For the space of a few years after the comet the whole throng of them stood around in a circle grieving together as one—and then they departed the scene, their role finished.

I often ponder that sad tableau, and alone in the quiet of an evening I sometimes suspect that those worthy cities did not die unmourned after all.

Appendix

THOSE WHO undertake to calculate the closest approach of Comet 1680 to the Earth's path for themselves will find that it missed by 77 earth-radii—not 62 as given in the text. The discrepancy stems from the fact that we are not so much interested in the path of the great comet itself as in the path of a fragment which moved initially in the same orbit but which followed by some 31 days and which might have struck the Earth. As it happened, this orbit lay fairly close to the ecliptic, and it was perturbed significantly by both Mars and Jupiter and especially by Saturn. Moreover, the interaction of Saturn upon an object following 31 days behind would have been even greater than upon the comet itself, and as a consequence the orbit of such a follower would have been pulled closer to the Earth's path by those 15 earth-radii.

In order to derive this result, the comet's path was integrated backwards from perihelion for about 43 years, or until it was judged that both the comet and its follower moved in the same Keplerian orbit about the mass center of the solar system. Then the time was increased by 31.356 days; the coordinate system was transformed back to one whose origin was at the mass center of the sun and four inner planets, and the direction of integration was reversed. Finally, the transformation back to heliocentric coordinates was effected about one year before perihelion.

As a formality perturbations from all the planets were taken into account, but only Mars, Jupiter and Saturn affected the differential motion appreciably. Positions of the outer planets were obtained by direct interpolation from the tables of Reference 10, taking into account all differences up to the 6th. This procedure was followed for the ten years prior to perihelion, then osculating elements were calculated to yield positions for earlier times. Obviously the representation became progressively poorer, but the error introduced by this approximation was small at worst, and the differential error between comet and follower was absolutely nil. Positions of the four inner planets were computed from elements appropriate to the epoch of perihelion of the comet derived from Newcomb's relations as given in Reference 28.

The calculation was performed to 10-digit precision using 6th difference integration formulae. The interval of integration was adjusted periodically to be as large as possible consistent with the requirement that the contribution of the 6th difference to the integral of acceleration be zero with margin to spare.

The aforementioned planetary interactions perturbed the path of the presumed companion comet in such a way that it intersected the earth's orbit about 18″ less in longitude than would otherwise be expected. Accordingly, the collision would have taken place at Julian Day No. 2,335,024.369, with the object approaching the Earth on a collision course from the point whose right ascension was $8^h 38^m$ and whose declination was 22.°1. The anti-point was therefore $20^h 38^m$ and -22.°1. The hour angle of the fictitious mean sun was 0.369 day or $8^h 51^m$; its right ascension was $18^h 9^m$, so the Greenwich siderial time was $3^h 00^m$. Therefore the anti-point was $6^h 23^m$ or about 96° west of Greenwich.

Bibliography

1: Baldwin, Percy M. (translator). *Discovery of the Seven Cities of Cibola,* by Fray Marcos de Niza. Historical Soc. of New Mexico, Publications in History, Vol. 1. Albuquerque: El Palacio Press, 1926.

2: Bartlett, Katharine and Colton, Harold S. "A note on the Marcos de Niza inscription near Phoenix, Arizona", Plateau, Vol. 12 (1940), 53-59.

3: Benham, James W. "Map of Salt River Valley, Arizona showing the location of Ancient Canals and Cities", Phoenix: Phoenix Free Museum, 1903.

4: Berg, L. S. "The origin of loess", Gerl. Beitr. Geophysik, Vol. 35 (1932), 130-150

5: Blacker, I. R. and Rosen, Harry M. *The Golden Conquistadores,* Indianapolis: Bobs-Merrill Co., 1960.

6: Bolton, Herbert Eugene. *Kino's Historical Memoir of Pimería Alta,* Cleveland: The Arthur H. Clark Co., 1919.

7: Burke, Rev. James T. *This Miserable Kingdom,* Santa Fe, New Mexico: Cristo Rey Church, 1973.

8: Burrus, Earnest J., S.J. (translator). *Kino Writes to the Duchess, Letters of Eusebio Francisco Kino, S.J. to the Duchess of Aveiro,* St. Louis, Mo.: St. Louis University, 1965.

9: Dos Passos, John, *Easter Island, Island of Enigmas,* Garden City, New York: Doubleday & Co., 1971.

10: Eckert, W. J., Brouwer, Dirk and Clemence, G. M. *Coordinates of the Five outer Planets 1653-2060,* Astron. Papers American Ephem. and Naut. Almanac, Washington D. C.: U. S. Government Printing Office, 1951.

11: Englert, Father Sebastian. *Island at the Center of the World,* New York: Charles Scribner's Sons, 1970.

12: Flammarion, Camille. *The Flammarion Book of Astronomy,* New York: Simon and Schuster, 1964.

13: Flint, Richard Foster. *Glacial and Quaternary Geology,* New York: John Wiley and Sons, 1971.

14: Gloucester HERALD (date not given), quoted in the Philosophical Magazine, Vol. 58 (1821), 310-311.

15: Fort, Charles. *The Book of the Damned,* New York: Ace Books (paperback).

16: Hallenbeck, Cleve. *The Journey of Fray Marcos de Niza,* Westport, Conn.: Greenwood Press, 1949.

17: Haury, Emil W. *The Hohokam, Desert Farmers and Craftsmen; Excavations at Snaketown 1964-1965,* Tucson: University of Arizona Press, 1976.

18: Hawley, F. G. "The manufacture of copper bells found in southwestern sites", Southwestern J. of Anthropology, Vol. 9 (1953), 99-111.

19: Holbert, C. M. *South Mountain and the Lost Cibola,* Phoenix: (privately printed pamphlet), 1938.

20: Howorth, H. H. "The loess—a rejoinder", Geol. Mag., Vol. 9 (1882), 343-356.

21: Karns, Harry J. (translator). *Unknown Arizona and Sonora,* from *Luz de Tierra Incognita,* by Captain Juan Mateo Manje, Tucson: Arizona Silhouettes, 1954.

22: Keilhack, K. "Das Rätsel der Lössbildung", Deut. geolog. Gesell. Zeit., Vol. 72 (1920), 146-161.

23: Kino, Eusebio Francisco, S.J. *Exposicion Astronomica de el Cometa Que el Ano de 1680, etc.,* Mexico City: 1681.

24: Lugn, A. L. "The origin of loesses and their relation to the Great Plains in North America" in Schultz, C. B. and Frye, J. C. (eds.), *Loess and Related Eolian Deposits of the World,* Lincoln: University of Nebraska Press, 1968.

25: Marsden, Brian G. *Catalogue of Cometary Orbits,* Second Edition, Cambridge: Smithsonian Astrophysical Observatory, 1975.

Selected References

26: Maziere, Francis. *Mysteries of Easter Island,* New York: W. W. Norton & Co., Inc., 1968.

27: Meek, A. "A shower of Sand-eels", Nature, Vol. 102 (1918), p. 46.

28: Métraux, Alfred. *Easter Island,* New York: Oxford University Press, 1957.

29: Nautical Almanac Offices. *Explanatory Supplement to the Astronomical Ephemeris and the American Ephemeris and Nautical Almanac,* London: Her Majesty's Stationery Office, 1961.

30: Patrick, H. R. *The Ancient Canal Systems and Pueblos of the Salt River Valley,* Arizona, Phoenix: The Phoenix Free Museum, 1903.

31: Phoenix, City of, Park Commission. Master Plan of Phoenix South Mountain Park, Map Number D-660-2 (4-10-1940).

32: Richthofen, Baron F. "On the mode of origin of the loess", Geol. Mag., Vol. 9 (1882), 293-305.

33: Ruhe, Robert V. *Quaternary Landscapes in Iowa,* Ames: Iowa State University Press, 1969.

34: San Franciso EXAMINER, Jan. 22, 1888; see also issues of Nov. 20 and Dec. 25 of 1887 and Jan. 1 of 1888.

35: Sauer, Carl. *The Road to Cibola,* Berkeley: University of California Press, 1932.

36: Simpson, General J. H. "Coronado's March in Search of the Seven Cities of Cibola & Discussion of their probable location", Smithsonian Institution Annual Report for 1869, Facsimile Reproduction by the Shorey Book Store, Seattle: 1968

37: Skertchly, S. B. and Kingsmill, T. W. "On the loess and other superficial deposits of Shantung (North China)" Quart. J. Geol. Soc., (London): Vol. 51 (1895), 238-254.

38: Skjölsvold, Arne. "The stone statues and quarries at Rano Raraku", in Heyerdahl, Thor and Ferdon, Edwin (eds.), *Archaeology of Easter Island,* Stockholm: Forum Publishing House, 1961.

39: Smith, Carlyle. "The Poike Ditch", in Heyerdahl, Thor and Ferdon, Edwin (eds.), *Archaeology of Easter Island,* Stockholm: Forum Publishing House, 1961.

40: Turney, Omar A. Map of Prehistoric Irrigation Canals, Phoenix, Arizona, 1922.

41: Turney, Omar A. "Prehistoric irrigation, II", Arizona Historical Review, Vol. 2 (1929), 11-52.

42: U. S. Geological Survey, Aerial Photograph 8-14-67; 1-148;GS-VBUL.

43: Willis, B., Blackwelder, E., and Sargent, R. H. *Research in China, I,* Washington, D. C.: Carnegie Institution, 1907.

44: Winchell, N. W. "The geology of Rock and Pipestone Counties", Ann. Report Geol. and Nat. Hist. Survey of Minnesota, Vol. 6 (1878), 93-111.

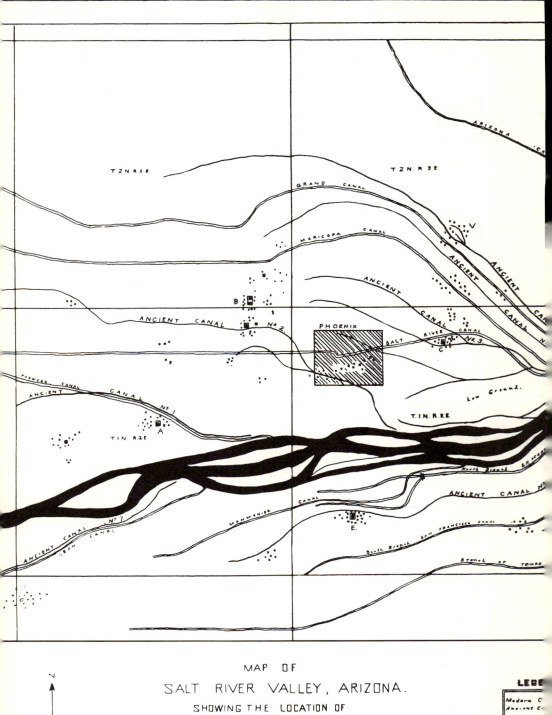

MAP OF

SALT RIVER VALLEY, ARIZONA.

SHOWING THE LOCATION OF

ANCIENT CANALS AND CITIES

FROM

EXPLORATIONS OF H.R.PATRICK.

PHOENIX ARIZONA.

1878 TO 1905.

N

LEGE

Modern C
Ancient Ca
Ruins of
Temples..
Ridges or
Township

River Cha
Scale of M